T0199998

Graphical User Interface Prototyping for Distributed Requirements Engineering

INFORMATIONSTECHNOLOGIE UND ÖKONOMIE

Herausgegeben von Christian Becker, Wolfgang Gaul,
Armin Heinzl, Alexander Mädche und Martin Schader

Band 54

Sven Scheibmayr

Graphical User Interface Prototyping for Distributed Requirements Engineering

Bibliographic Information published by the Deutsche Nationalbibliothek
The Deutsche Nationalbibliothek lists this publication
in the Deutsche Nationalbibliografie; detailed bibliographic
data is available in the internet at http://dnb.d-nb.de.

Zugl.: Mannheim, Univ., Diss., 2013

Library of Congress Cataloging-in-Publication Data
Scheibmayr, Sven, 1980-
Graphical user interface prototyping for distributed requirements engineering /
Sven Scheibmayr.
pages cm. — (Informationstechnologie und Ökonomie, ISSN 1616-086X)
Includes bibliographical references.
ISBN 978-3-631-65094-3 — ISBN 978-3-653-04315-0 (E-book) 1. Graphical
user interfaces (Computer systems) 2. software engineering. 3. Prototypes,
Engineering. 4. Electronic data processing—Distributed processing. I.Title.
QA76.9.U83S37 2014
005.4'37—dc 3

2014006553

D 180
ISSN 1616-086X
ISBN 978-3-631-65094-3 (Print)
E-ISBN 978-3-653-04315-0 (E-Book)
DOI 10.3726/978-3-653-04315-0

© Peter Lang GmbH
Internationaler Verlag der Wissenschaften
Frankfurt am Main 2014
All rights reserved.
PL Academic Research is an Imprint of Peter Lang GmbH.

Peter Lang – Frankfurt am Main · Bern · Bruxelles · New York ·
Oxford · Warszawa · Wien

This book is part of an editor's series of PL Academic Research
and was peer reviewed prior to publication.
www.peterlang.com

Acknowledgments

This doctoral thesis has been an exciting and challenging project. A lot of people were involved and contributed to it. In the following, I want to thank them for their support and contributions.

First and foremost, I want to express my gratitude to my doctoral adviser Professor Dr. Armin Heinzl for letting me begin this journey and supporting me on my way. He gave me the freedom to work on the questions that I found most compelling and shape this research project according to my desires. His support and his essential advice guided my efforts into the right direction.

Furthermore, I want to thank Professor Dr. Irene Bertschek, Professor Dr. Christian Becker, and Professor Dr. Wolfgang Effelsberg who were members of my examination committee.

When I was conducting the evaluation part of this thesis, I had the opportunity to interview several industry experts. I owe them a debt of gratitude for sharing their knowledge with me. They contributed valuable insights and data, which show the usefulness of the artifacts I developed.

Moreover, I want to thank my great colleagues and former colleagues from our chair. They supported me in every aspect of my work. I always enjoyed the supportive and pleasant atmosphere at the chair, the countless discussions, and the fun.

Finally, I want to express my profound gratitude for the support of my friends and my family. They encouraged me and provided advice in all the challenging situations that I had to manage. In particular, I want to thank my parents, who enabled me to pursue my ambitions.

Mannheim, April 2013   Sven Scheibmayr

Contents

List of Figures

List of Tables

List of Abbreviations

API	Application Programming Interface
CRM	Customer Relationship Management
CSS	Cascading Style Sheets
DOM	Document Object Model
GUI	Graphical User Interface
HTML	Hypertext Markup Language
HTTP	Hypertext Transfer Protocol
IEEE	Institute of Electrical and Electronics Engineers
IT	Information Technology
JSON	JavaScript Object Notation
MVC	Model-View-Controller
OMG	Object Management Group
PDF	Portable Document Format
PHP	PHP: Hypertext Preprocessor
RE	Requirements Engineering
SE	Software Engineering
SRS	Software Requirements Specification

SVG   Scalable Vector Graphics

TCP   Transmission Control Protocol

UI   User Interface

UML   Unified Modeling Language

URL   Uniform Resource Locator

VML   Vector Markup Language

W3C   Word Wide Web Consortium

XML   Extensible Markup Language

1. Introduction

1.1. Problem Outline

The objective of Software Engineering (SE) is to build high quality software within a given time and with a predetermined budget (Sommerville, 2007). Often, though, software development projects still struggle to accomplish these objectives and many fail (Charette, 2005; The Standish Group, 2009). Studies show that in many cases, problems in the early phase of software development lead to cost or time overruns, rework, bad quality, and eventually to the failure of the project (Procaccino et al., 2006; Hofmann and Lehner, 2001).

Requirements Engineering (RE) is the phase of SE which deals with this early phase of software development (Sommerville and Sawyer, 1997; Nuseibeh and Easterbrook, 2000). RE can be defined as follows: "Requirements engineering is the disciplined application of proven principles, methods, tools, and notations to describe a proposed system's intended behavior and its associated constraints"(Hsia et al., 1993). RE comprises activities such as the elicitation of the requirements, their specification, and their management. The main task of RE is essentially the transfer of knowledge between stakeholders in the project and the creation of a common understanding of "what to build". Stakeholders are individuals or organizations which actively participate in a software project or whose interests influence the project (Hofmann and Lehner, 2001).

Today, globalization also affects the processes of how software is built and many development projects nowadays are conducted in globally distributed

environments, where project stakeholders are spread over multiple locations
and often work in different time zones (Karolak, 1998). This distribution of
stakeholders leads to a variety of challenges in collaboration and communication
(Herbsleb and Moitra, 2001) and needs for research in that field (Hargreaves
et al., 2004). Stakeholders are not able to communicate in the same way as in
face-to-face meetings at one location. Informal and ad-hoc communication is
impeded[1].

Synchronous rich communication needs significant effort and tools. Furthermore, multiple time-zones often constrain the available time for synchronous
communication. Cultural differences and language barriers make communication and collaboration more difficult. As RE requires extensive communication,
these problems make it even more challenging in global and distributed projects.
To ensure an efficient and effective communication over distance, solid methods
and tools have to be developed and evaluated. The design of these methods
and tools should be informed by existing theoretical knowledge about communication and coordination processes in order to ensure the effectiveness of these
methods and tools (Hevner et al., 2004).

This thesis focuses on the following general question:

*"How can it be ensured that requirements engineering leads to high
quality requirements in distributed software development projects?"*

The general objective of this research is to support requirements engineering
to come up with requirements in such a way that the system to be build meets
the stakeholders' needs. The search for these requirements is usually conducted
in the elicitation and analysis phase of requirements engineering (Sommerville,

---

1 Many popular agile software development methodologies, which try to solve common problems of traditional methodologies, e.g. Scrum (Schwaber, 2004), have been developed for
co-located stakeholders.

2007), which is the main research focus of this work. Elicitation deals with discovering the needs of all relevant stakeholders (Hickey and Davis, 2004). These needs lead to requirements, which are collected and further analyzed. The analysis activities comprise classification, prioritization, and negotiation of requirements. Different objectives of different stakeholders must be taken into account.

Requirements elicitation and analysis are activities, which often cannot be considered separately because of their highly iterative nature (Geisser, 2008). In agile software development, these activities are even more intertwined, overlapping and are repeated because agile development processes imply iterative activities (Lee and Xia, 2010; Paetsch et al., 2003). Requirements elicitation and analysis are communication-intense and critical activities in software development projects (Zowghi and Coulin, 2005). They concentrate on the task of finding out *"what problem needs to be solved"* rather than on *"how the problem should be solved"* (Nuseibeh and Easterbrook, 2000). Due to the required communication intensity of these activities and the fact that stakeholders are located at different places and possibly reside within different cultural environments, these activities are even more difficult.

1.2. Research Focus and Objective

The research objective of this work is to develop a method and a software artifact to support the activities in the early requirements engineering phase in order to overcome some of the difficulties and improve the quality of the requirements, which should eventually lead to better software products. There are many techniques, which can be used in this early phase, to elicit requirements in software development, e.g. brainstorming, interviews, business process modeling or observation (Zowghi and Coulin, 2005). A technique which has been

shown to be very effective in this phase is graphical user interface (GUI) prototyping (Gomaa and Scott, 1981; Bäumer et al., 1996; Newman and Landay,
2000; Ravid and Berry, 2000). For instance, in a study by Keil and Carmel
(1995), GUI prototyping was one of the most effective customer-developer link.
GUI prototypes are also popular in practice, especially in agile projects as they
are quickly created and convey ideas without a lot of documentation. The prototypes show characteristics which makes GUI prototyping a promising technique
for knowledge transfer between stakeholders (see Section 3.1.1). Hence, GUI
prototypes have been chosen as the research focus of this thesis.

These prototypes, also known as mockups, help to visualize the system which
has to be build, support the users of this system to get a clearer picture of their
requirements, and serve as a tool to quickly try out various ideas and functionalities. They are an early representation of the user-visible part of the system
and help to provide a common understanding of the requirements of the system, both on the developer and the user side, and improve the usability of the
product (Arnowitz et al., 2007). User interface prototypes exist on a multitude
of sophistication levels: from simple, paper-based sketches to dynamic functional graphical user interfaces created with heavy weighted interface creation
applications (Rudd et al., 1996). Especially in the very first phase of the development, often simple, paper-based prototypes are used in order to visualize
and try out ideas quickly (Chamberlain et al., 2006).

As prototypes are means to convey design ideas and help stakeholders to get a
common understanding of the requirements, GUI prototyping also seems to be
a promising approach in *distributed* software engineering, where communication
and knowledge management problems are even more striking than in co-located
settings. Prototyping can help distributed stakeholders in the early phase of
development to get a common understanding of the requirements of the software
product and the business context. Prototypes facilitate the communication of

stakeholders, who are situated in different locations, with different professional and cultural environments.

Furthermore, research in this area is of high relevance as prototyping is a common technique in agile development (Paetsch et al., 2003) and there are attempts to use agile development methods also in distributed environments (Ramesh et al., 2006; Hildenbrand, 2008). Nevertheless, little research has been conducted so far in the application of GUI prototyping in distributed software development. However, for the effective application of this technique, methods and tools for the collaboration on user interface prototypes over distance are needed. When designing such methods and tools, theoretical knowledge should be utilized to make them more effective. The objective of this thesis is the design and implementation of such a method and tool. The design should be informed by theory and the resulting artifacts be evaluated for their effectiveness and efficiency.

This objective leads to the following research questions:

1. How can GUI prototypes be collaboratively created, shared, maintained, and integrated into the distributed development process?

2. What kind of tool should be applied?

3. Does this approach help the stakeholders to better understand the requirements and collaborate more efficiently?

Question one focuses on a method for distributed GUI prototyping. Such a method should provide guidelines on how to create the prototypes and collaborate on them from various distributed locations, how to use prototypes of different levels of detail and functionality, and how to integrate the prototypes with other artifacts into the distributed development process. This question will be answered in Section 4.1.

The second question is related to the tool which is required to implement this method. This tool must provide the functionality that is required by the method. Beyond the design implications, which are derived from theoretical considerations and practical requirements, technical design decisions for the implementation have to be made. This question will be answered in Section 4.2.

Question three indicates that one objective of this research is to support stakeholders in the understanding of the software requirements. Furthermore, the collaboration between the stakeholders should become more efficient. To assess if the developed artifacts improve the understanding and the efficiency, they are evaluated. Chapter 5 describes this evaluation and reports its results and thus answers question three.

1.3. Research Method

To answer the questions stated in the previous section, this research will follow a design science research method (March and Smith, 1995; Hevner et al., 2004). This approach is based on a problem solving paradigm (Hevner et al., 2004). The goal is to solve the problem presented above. It is the support and improvement of user interface prototyping in globally distributed software development. To achieve this goal, two artifacts are designed, which address the problem.

The artifacts are a method and a tool, which support stakeholders in globally distributed software projects to collaborate on GUI prototypes. Following the design science approach, this research draws from existing literature and is informed by theoretical concepts, which are used for the creation of the purposeful artifacts (Hevner et al., 2004; Markus et al., 2002). These theoretical concepts are described in Section 3.1. The theoretical knowledge is used to derive design implications for the artifacts. Further design implications from practice are determined by conducting expert interviews. These design implications are described in Section 3.2. After collecting the design implications, the artifacts are constructed. For the tool, further technical design decisions are made and the tool is implemented as a software application.

For the artifacts, which are the contributions of this research, to be purposeful, they must provide utility, which must be assessed (Hevner et al., 2004). For this purpose, the utility, quality, and efficiency of the artifacts are evaluated with well-established evaluation methods. This evaluation provides feedback for the construction of the artifact. The two artifacts of this research will be evaluated by the means of expert interviews. This is described in Chapter 5.

1.4. Organization of this Thesis

The rest of this thesis is structured as follows: Chapter 2 introduces fundamental concepts, which are important for the understanding of this research. It explains Requirements Engineering and its activities, the challenges of software engineering in distributed environments, GUI prototypes, and design science research. After this, related research is described.

Chapter 3 uses theoretical knowledge to derive design implications for the artifacts. First, the concept of boundary objects and the two theoretical concepts, the Cognitive-Affective Model of Organizational Communication for Designing Information Technology (IT) and the Media Synchronicity Theory, are introduced. After this, design implications are derived and preliminary assessed by experts from the software industry. Finally, existing tools are analyzed and it is checked if they meet the requirements of the design implications.

Chapter 4 outlines in detail the artifacts that have been developed: a method and tool for distributed GUI prototyping. The method, its steps, and example scenarios are described. Subsequently, the tool, its usage, its technologies, and its architecture are explained in detail.

In Chapter 5, the evaluation of the artifacts developed earlier is described. First, the context of the evaluation is introduced and two propositions are derived. Thereupon, the design of the evaluation is described and its results are reported.

Chapter 6 discusses the contributions, the implications and the limitations of this work. Finally, Chapter 7 offers a summary of this thesis and an outlook for future research.

2. Foundations

This chapter introduces fundamental topics and concepts, which are important for the understanding of this thesis. As this research is concerned with the determination of the requirements when a new software system is to be build, *requirements engineering* as a discipline is introduced in Section 2.1. When a software development team is distributed, problems come up and require dedicated solutions. This research explicitly deals with software development in distributed settings. Thus, this topic is introduced in Section 2.2. The main topic of this thesis is the usage of graphical user interface prototypes as a technique for the elicitation and analysis of requirements. In Section 2.3 prototyping and its different types and advantages are discussed. Section 2.4 introduces design science research, which is the research method of this work. Finally, Section 2.5 discusses related research to illustrate the research gap that is filled by this work.

2.1. Requirements Engineering

2.1.1. Requirements Engineering as a Discipline in Software Development

When a new software system is developed, dealing with its requirements is crucial for the success of the project (van Lamsweerde, 2000; Aurum and Wohlin, 2005b). In the development process, this is one of the first and most important steps, as all further development tasks depend on correct requirements (Hofmann and Lehner, 2001). Requirements engineering deals with the elicitation, analysis, and management of requirements (Kotonya and Sommerville, 1998). Requirements describe what a system should do and which functionalities it should contain. Furthermore, constraints and boundary conditions of a system are defined (Sommerville and Sawyer, 1997). Many different definitions for *requirements* exist in literature (see Sommerville and Sawyer, 1997; Leffingwell and Widrig, 2000). An often cited definition for requirements is provided by the Institute of Electrical and Electronics Engineers (IEEE) and also used by Loucopoulos and Karakostas (1995), Hofmann (2000), and Aurum and Wohlin (2005b):

"Requirement.

1. *A condition or capacity needed by a user to solve a problem or achieve an objective.*

2. *A condition or capability that must be met or possessed by a system or system component to satisfy a contract, standard, specification or other formally imposed documents.*

3. *A documented representation of a condition or capability as in 1 or 2"* (IEEE, 1990, p.62).

This definition, which is also used for this thesis, shows that requirements do not only refer to user needs but can also be derived from formal standards or specifications, which have to be met. One example is a standard or specification which is required by the government. Another one is an industrial standard which is contractually required between the client and the development organization (Aurum and Wohlin, 2005b).

Requirements ideally describe *"what"* a system should do and not *"how"* it gets realized, but often, there are differences how people in software development projects interpret what *"what"* exactly means (Aurum and Wohlin, 2005b). Hence, the fact that requirements should not refer to how the system works has been discussed for a long time. Research generally supports this idea, whereas practitioners see requirements and design as interrelated (Berry and Lawrence, 1998).

The requirements for a system to be developed have to be discovered, analyzed, documented and managed. All these activities are part of *requirements engineering* (Kotonya and Sommerville, 1998). There are many different definitions for requirements engineering in literature (Pohl, 1997). As an example Hsia et al. (1993) define requirements engineering as follows:

> *"Requirements engineering is the disciplined application of proven principles, methods, tools, and notations to describe a proposed system's intended behavior and its associated constraints"* (Hsia et al., 1993, p.75).

Another, slightly different definition is given by Aurum and Wohlin (2005b):

> *"Requirements engineering is concerned with the identification of goals for a proposed system, the operation and conversion of these goals into services and constraints, as well as the assignment of responsibilities for the resulting requirements to agents such as humans, devices and software"* (Aurum and Wohlin, 2005b, p.2).

This definition is more specific than the one by Hsia et al. (1993) and relates requirements engineering to the goals for a system. Furthermore, it refers to the assignment of responsibilities for the requirements, e.g. assigning requirements to persons, who could be software developers.

Traditional plan-driven software development projects with a waterfall process reserve their first phases for requirements engineering. In such projects, all subsequent phases, like design, implementation, and testing, build upon this first phase and are only executed when this first phase is finished (Royce, 1970; Kotonya and Sommerville, 1998).

In the recent years, agile software development methods have become popular (Lindvall et al., 2002; Nerur et al., 2005). In agile development projects, the development is conducted in cycles. Hence, requirements engineering activities often occur throughout the whole process (Cao and Ramesh, 2008; Aurum and Wohlin, 2005a). But even in these agile projects, all design and implementation activities depend on the requirements, as they define the behavior of the software.

As the term requirements *engineering* illustrates, requirements engineering is an engineering discipline and a sub-discipline of *software engineering*. Software engineering is a discipline that systematically uses principles, techniques, methods, and tools to develop software (Sommerville and Sawyer, 1997). Its characteristic is, that it approaches a development problem as an engineering problem. Requirements engineering also follows this systematic approach (van Lamsweerde, 2000). The following definition of Loucopoulos and Karakostas (1995) emphasizes this fact:

> *"Requirements engineering (RE) can be defined as the systematic process of developing requirements through an iterative co-operative process of analyzing the problem, documenting the resulting observations in a variety of representation formats, and checking the accuracy of the understanding gained"* (Loucopoulos and Karakostas, 1995, p.13).

This definition also reflects the collaborative nature of requirements engineering. Requirements engineering needs the coordinated work of many people from different domains, so-called stakeholders (Crowston and Kammerer, 1998;

Loucopoulos and Karakostas, 1995). Stakeholders are individuals or organizations which actively participate in a software project or whose interests influence the project (Hofmann and Lehner, 2001). They could comprise, for instance, customers, users, developers, business analysts or project managers. In many cases, stakeholders use the new system or have knowledge which is essential for its development (Robertson and Robertson, 2000). Furthermore, organizations providing regulatory requirements, like governmental organizations, can be stakeholders (Kotonya and Sommerville, 1998). For requirements engineering to be successful, it is important to identify all relevant stakeholders who can contribute knowledge from different domains.

This knowledge has to be collected, transferred, and integrated in order to specify the requirements, which needs a lot of communication. The coordination and collaboration of the various stakeholders, who often have contradicting needs during requirements engineering, is challenging (Hsieh, 2006). Especially when stakeholders are distributed at different locations in global software engineering projects, the collaboration is complicated, as the interaction and communication between the stakeholders is difficult (Damian, 2007) (see Section 2.2). The collaborative nature of requirements engineering is even more distinct in agile projects than in traditional plan-driven development projects, as stakeholders interact more closely, in order to react faster to changes. Everyone in the agile team collaborates with the customer in order to understand the requirements (Chau et al., 2003).

The previous definition of Loucopoulos and Karakostas (1995) refers to different representations of requirements. These representations can be diverse. Informal textual descriptions exist as well as requirements modeled with formal languages (Loucopoulos and Karakostas, 1995). Another representation are prototypes of graphical user interfaces, which are the main research topic of this thesis and will be described in Section 2.3.

Requirements engineering is one of the most difficult parts in a software development project (Hofmann and Lehner, 2001; Wiegers, 2006). As Fred Brooks already wrote in his well-known paper in 1987:

> *"The hardest single part of building a software system is deciding precisely what to build. No other part of the conceptual work is as difficult as establishing the detailed technical requirements, including all the interfaces to people, to machines, and to other software systems. No other part of the work so cripples the resulting system if done wrong. No other part is more difficult to rectify later. Therefore, the most important function that the software builder performs for the client is the iterative extraction and refinement of the product requirements"* (Brooks, 1987, p.17).

There are many factors which contribute to the challenges in requirements engineering (Wiegers, 2003). Requirements are difficult to uncover as no single stakeholder can imagine the whole system in its entirety with all its details (Hsia et al., 1993). Hence, the description of the system is most often incomplete and seldom fully understood (Berry and Lawrence, 1998). Often trial and error is used, when specifying the requirements. Requirements are changed and added as the stakeholders begin to understand the system better (Hsia et al., 1993). Moreover, requirements are not mere facts which are delivered by the stakeholders. Requirements have to be negotiated (Herlea and Greenberg, 1998). In these negotiations, many stakeholders from various domains with different knowledge and diverse and often conflicting interests and goals participate. This can lead to conflicts, which have to be solved (van Lamsweerde, 2000; Nuseibeh and Easterbrook, 2000).

The problem gets more difficult for large software systems (Bergman et al., 2002). When a large software system is developed, the number of stakeholders and the number of domains can be huge. This leads to a enormous amount of requirements, which have to be complete and consistent. No single person can manage this huge number of requirements (Crowston and Kammerer, 1998). A further problem is that stakeholders have different backgrounds and vocabularies. It is difficult for them to communicate and come to a shared understanding about the software requirements. For instance, users often prefer natural language while developers prefer formal descriptions, which users struggle to understand (Hsia et al., 1993; Crowston and Kammerer, 1998).

Requirements engineering is challenging, but it is also extremely important for the success of a software project (Hofmann, 2000; Glass, 1998). Unstable requirements are one of the most frequent reasons for project failures (Glass, 2001). The quality of the software depends hugely on the requirements. When the requirements are incorrect, incomplete or ambiguous, developers are not able to acquire the knowledge to build the right system and customers cannot determine what they should expect from the system (Hsia et al., 1993). Furthermore, errors made during requirements engineering are most common and most expensive to correct (Aurum and Wohlin, 2005b). It is estimated that the cost to correct these errors when coding has already begun, is five to ten times higher than during the requirements engineering phase and that the cost is 100 to 200 times higher when the software has already been shipped and is in use (Boehm, 1981).

Verner et al. (2005) conducted a study with 164 software projects and examined the relation of requirements engineering and software project success. They found that high quality requirements and the effective management of those are most important for project success. Furthermore, the involvement of customers and users is crucial to come to these high quality requirements and contributes highly to the success of the project (Verner et al., 2005). Hall et al. (2002) collected data from nearly 200 subjects in twelve software companies. They discovered that 48 % of all development problems that were stated by the subjects were related to requirements. Furthermore, they showed that almost two thirds of the requirements problems were related to organizational problems and 36 of those problems were communication problems (Hall et al., 2002).

Also Hofmann and Lehner (2001) show that requirements engineering is a critical success factor in software development projects. Their data from fifteen teams with in total 76 stakeholders shows that the projects which devoted considerably more effort to requirements engineering were more successful. Furthermore, a decisive factor in the most successful projects was the involvement of users and customers during requirements engineering (Hofmann and Lehner, 2001). As requirements are seen more and more important in software development projects, also requirements engineering becomes increasingly an essential research topic in software engineering and in the field of information systems[1] (Aurum and Wohlin, 2005b).

2.1.2. Requirements Engineering Process

Requirements engineering can be seen as a process, which can be subdivided into several phases. Kotonya and Sommerville (1998) describe four different phases: *requirements elicitation, requirements analysis and negotiation, requirements documentation, requirements validation.* Other authors also use these terms (Scacchi, 2002; Nuseibeh and Easterbrook, 2000; Wiegers, 2003). The phases can be structured in a purely linear way, like in Macaulay (1996). This is shown in Figure 2.1. Another possibility is an iterative process with cycles, which is proposed by Kotonya and Sommerville (1998) and Wiegers (2003). Furthermore, a fifth activity, *requirements management,* exists, which is con-

---

1 See Section 2.5 for related research conducted on requirements engineering.

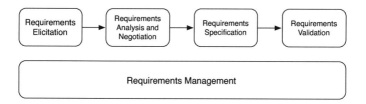

Figure 2.1.: Requirements Engineering Phases

cerned with the management of requirements changes and is conducted during the whole requirements engineering process (Sommerville and Sawyer, 1997).

2.1.2.1. Requirements Elicitation

One of the most essential phases in the requirements engineering process is the requirements elicitation phase (Hickey and Davis, 2004). In most processes, it is the first activity, which all other activities depend on (Loucopoulos and Karakostas, 1995). Requirements elicitation deals with the identification of the user and customer needs (Hsia et al., 1993). All stakeholders who have relevant knowledge should collaborate closely in this phase to determine the requirements which the system should fulfill (Sommerville, 2007). Requirements elicitation is very communication-intense as many stakeholders have to deliver their input and a lot of knowledge has to be transferred (Coughlan and Macredie, 2002).

Software developers have to be familiar with the working environment of the users. They have to understand how users of the software work, which needs they have, and which restrictions they are subjected to (Sommerville, 2007; Dieste et al., 2008). The application domain and the business environment has to be understood (Sommerville, 2005). Moreover, customer representatives and users have to learn what to expect from the system and have to clearly state their needs (Saiedian and Dale, 2000). There are many techniques which can be used for requirements elicitation (Hickey and Davis, 2004). Sommerville (2007) mentions e.g., interviews, viewpoints, scenarios, and prototyping. For a detailed overview and description of these and other widely used techniques and approaches for requirements elicitation see Zowghi and Coulin (2005).

The elicitation of requirements is a demanding and complex task. There are various issues which can lead to errors, delays, and rework (Sommerville, 2007). Among these issues are communication problems. In many cases, stakeholders have difficulties to express their expectations (Zowghi and Coulin, 2005). Stakeholders are often experts in their business and have accumulated a lot of knowledge which is hard to explain and transfer to others (Nuseibeh and Easterbrook, 2000). Stakeholders from different domains use different terms and expressions and use concepts which are not directly understandable by the other party (Coughlan et al., 2003). Furthermore, it is challenging for users or customers to estimate what is feasible, thus requirements can be unrealistic or new innovative solutions can be overlooked (Zowghi and Coulin, 2005).

Another issue is that software systems are often very complex, with many interdependent requirements and involve a multitude of stakeholders (Saiedian and Dale, 2000). This leads to communication overhead and can result in many conflicting requirements (van Lamsweerde et al., 1998). Additionally, political issues and conflicting interests can arise, as stakeholders follow personal interests and try to influence requirements decisions (Bergman et al., 2002). Furthermore, motivating stakeholders to dedicate time and effort and contribute their knowledge to the elicitation of requirements can sometimes be difficult, because stakeholders might view these activities as a disruption of their daily work and additional overhead (Robertson and Robertson, 2000).

2.1.2.2. Requirements Analysis and Negotiation

In this phase, requirements elicited in the first phase are analyzed and negotiated in order to decide which requirements enter the specification (Kotonya
and Sommerville, 1998). As the input of many stakeholders is included during
the elicitation phase, conflicts and inconsistencies between the requirements can
emerge (van Lamsweerde et al., 1998). They can be contradicting, overlapping,
incomplete, ambiguous or unrealistic (Sommerville and Sawyer, 1997). These
problems have to be resolved during the requirements analysis and negotiation
phase. Stakeholders discuss the issues, come up with a common understanding of the requirements, and negotiate trade-offs between different requirements
(Bergman et al., 2002).

Furthermore, in many cases a large number of requirements is elicited but
development resources are limited (Robertson and Robertson, 2006). Therefore, the prioritization of requirements is often needed (Berander and Andrews,
2005). Prioritization of requirements is possible if they are not of equal importance, which is often the case. There can be huge differences between the
customer value which each requirement contributes when it is implemented
(Karlsson, 1996). Some requirements are critical as the utility of the system
would be diminished to a large extend, if they were not implemented. Others
are less important, as they are desirable but not essential. Therefore, the most
important requirements have to be selected and implemented first. In order to
select these requirements, several criteria can be examined, e.g.: utility, cost,
and risk (Berander and Andrews, 2005). Several methods to prioritize requirements have been developed. Examples are the Planning Game, which is used in
Extreme Programming (Beck, 1999) and the Cost-Value Approach by Karlsson
and Ryan (1997).

2.1.2.3. Requirements Specification

After requirements have been elicited, analyzed and negotiated, they are specified. For that purpose, formal or informal notations can be used (Fraser et al.,
1991). Examples for a formal notation are a structured language or standardized
forms, as proposed by Sommerville (2007). Furthermore, logical and mathematical notations can be used (Wiegers, 2003). Furthermore, informal notations
like natural language are widely used in the industry today (Denger et al.,
2003). Another possibility to specify requirements are graphical notations, e.g.,
graphical user interface prototypes (see Section 2.3).

The requirements specification phase results in one ore more documents,
which contain the specified requirements and describe the behavior of the system and its constraints (Hsia et al., 1993). These documents are called software
requirements specifications (SRS) (Wiegers, 2003). Several attempts exist to
standardize the SRS documents. For instance, the IEEE developed the IEEE
standard 830-1998 (IEEE, 1998), which defines a structure for an SRS document and defines several criteria to ensure the quality of the specification. Another template is developed for the Volere method by Robertson and Robertson
(2006). Furthermore use cases, which are standardized in the Unified Modeling
Language (UML) by the Object Management Group (OMG)[2], can be used in
SRS documents (Cockburn, 2000).

2.1.2.4. Requirements Validation

As a last step in the requirements engineering process, the specified requirements are validated. Requirements validation should ensure that the requirements fit with the users' needs and specify exactly what the users expect the

---

2 http://www.omg.org/ (accessed 03/04/2012)

system to do (Sommerville, 2007). Flaws in the specification, like ambiguities or invalid requirements, are eliminated (Wiegers, 2003). When requirements are ambiguous, there are several possible interpretations for their meaning, which can lead to wrong implementations (Kamsties, 2005). Requirements can be invalid, when they contradict each other or the requirements are not implementable (Gervasi and Zowghi, 2005; Hofmann, 2000). Also incomplete requirements should be corrected.

Furthermore, requirements should be verifiable. This means that it can be shown through testing that the implementation meets the requirements (Sommerville, 2007). Essential quality criteria for requirements, which can be used during validation, can be found in the IEEE standard 830-1998 (IEEE, 1998). It is important to note that finding and correcting errors in the requirements as early as possible is crucial. Finding and correcting errors later in the process, e.g., after the implementation of the software, is of magnitudes more costly than during the requirements validation phase.

There are several techniques for the validation of requirements. Sommerville (2007) describes reviews, prototyping, test-case generation and automated consistency analysis. During requirements reviews, stakeholders from the developer and customer side check manually the quality criteria of the requirements and their mutual understanding of the requirements. With prototypes, stakeholders can test, if the defined requirements meet their needs and if they were properly understood (see Section 2.3). Test-cases can be used in a similar way and allow to estimate the implementation complexity of a requirement. If requirements are specified with a formal notation, software tools can be used to automatically check the requirements for their consistency (Sommerville, 2007).

2.1.2.5. Requirements Management

Requirements management is an activity which is conducted concurrently during all the other phases described above (Sommerville, 2007). As requirements changes occur very often during software development projects, keeping track of these changes and managing them is part of this activity (Kotonya and Sommerville, 1998). Requirements changes can occur because the understanding of the user needs and the views of the customers and the developers change (Hsia et al., 1993). Furthermore, the economic context or regulatory rules can change during the project. To manage these changes, a process should be defined which the change requests have to go through (Wiegers, 2003). The impact of changes to requirements on other requirements and system components has to be analyzed (Gotel and Finkelstein, 1994). This helps project managers to estimate the costs of a requirement change. For that purpose, dependencies must be traceable.

2.2. Distributed and Collaborative Software Engineering

In the recent years, a trend has emerged that many software development projects involve stakeholders who are distributed between several locations around the globe (Hsieh, 2006). There are several reasons for this trend towards globally distributed software development. On reason is a lack of resources at one location. As software gets increasingly complex and knowledge gets more and more specialized, often more qualified staff is needed than available locally (Kommeren and Parviainen, 2007). Furthermore, costs for developers at different locations differ significantly. These differences can be utilized when developers are hired in low wage countries, which is often stated as one of the major reasons for offshoring projects (Dibbern et al., 2008). Also the potential to work around the clock, handing over the work from one time zone to the other – the so called follow-the-sun approach – is seen as an advantage (Conchúir et al., 2009). As software is a virtual good and can be exchanged via computer networks, the collaboration of many stakeholders at different locations is possible (Espinosa et al., 2002).

On the one hand, there are many reasons for globally distributed software development, but one the other hand distributed settings also involve a multitude of challenges (Redmiles et al., 2007). The separation between stakeholders affects communication. Informal communication, which would happen frequently in co-located environments (e.g. the so called "water cooler talk"), is missing almost completely (Damian, 2007). Moreover, communication is less rich than in co-located teams and response times are longer (Espinosa et al., 2002). As team members share a lot of context about their work with the help of informal communication, there is a lack of awareness for the other team members work in distributed settings (Kommeren and Parviainen, 2007). Furthermore, the communication problems lead to difficulties in the coordination of tasks (Espinosa et al., 2007b).

It is not only the spatial distance between stakeholders which causes challenges in communication, but also the fact that team members are often located in different time-zones and, thus, have little overlap in working time (Sengupta et al., 2006). This leads to delays in communication. Other reasons for problems in globally distributed projects are due to cultural and social differences (Redmiles et al., 2007). These differences complicate the collaboration as the problem-solving and communication processes differ (Hsieh, 2006). Language and trust-related issues are also relevant and hamper collaboration (Kommeren and Parviainen, 2007). Further problems are strategic issues, knowledge management issues, process management issues and technical issues (Herbsleb and Moitra, 2001).

Sengupta et al. (2006) describe the strategic issue of distributing work across development locations most effectively and reasonably. Knowledge management is hindered as communication becomes more difficult, which slows down knowledge sharing (Damian, 2007). If development processes are not aligned between different sites, this can lead to synchronization and integration issues (Sengupta et al., 2006). Furthermore, technical problems as connectivity and bandwidth-related issues can occur (Sengupta et al., 2006). All these issues of globally distributed software projects have been reported in several empirical studies (e.g., Boland and Fitzgerald, 2004; Kommeren and Parviainen, 2007; Jiménez et al., 2009).

The challenges in such projects impact productivity and quality negatively (Ramasubbu and Balan, 2007). A significant amount of development time is spent on overhead, which means that additional project management, coordination, and communication activities are needed (Kommeren and Parviainen, 2007). A study by Herbsleb and Mockus (2003) showed that in distributed settings, the completion of work packages took more than two times as long as comparable work packages in co-located teams.

All the issues in globally distributed software development projects described above are especially relevant in the area of distributed requirements engineering. As requirements engineering is very communication intense and needs frequent interaction between stakeholders, it is significantly more challenging in distributed projects (Damian, 2007). Komi-Sirviö and Tihinen (2005) conducted a study about distributed software development and asked individuals in 21 organizations. The respondents stressed problems related to requirements engineering and ranked misinterpretation of requirements in distributed projects as the most important reason for errors (Komi-Sirviö and Tihinen, 2005).

Several researchers suggest approaches to alleviate the problems in globally distributed software development projects. Damian (2007) proposes that a method for distributed requirements engineering should consider three kinds processes: processes for knowledge sharing and acquisition; iterative processes, which help the stakeholders to frequently check if their understanding of the requirements are still valid; and coordination and communication processes, which facilitate the other two kinds of processes.

Redmiles et al. (2007) suggest a continuous coordination approach, which tries to combine formal and informal coordination mechanisms. It provides formal checkpoints but also fosters informal communication to support awareness of the stakeholders for each others work (Redmiles et al., 2007). Jiménez et al. (2009) list several success factors for distributed software projects: e.g. training of team members in the relevant processes and tools; tracking of issues, tasks and people assigned to those in order to provide awareness of development activities; use of source code version control system; using metrics to measure performance indicators systematically.

Espinosa et al. (2007a) examined the impact of team familiarity in software development projects and showed that the positive effect of familiarity of the team members is stronger when team members are globally distributed. Hence, it is recommended to increase team familiarity in distributed projects. Measures which help to do that are e.g., business trips of team members to other locations; building teams with members which previously worked together; and the use of video conferencing technologies (Espinosa et al., 2002, 2007a). Espinosa et al. (2007b) recommend to advocate methods and tools which enhance the knowledge about the team members' work and their presence awareness.

Geisser and Hildenbrand (2006) developed a method for globally distributed requirements engineering, which supports this knowledge sharing in distributed teams. It realizes this by using a Wiki for collaborative requirements elicitation and a web-based work item tracking system (Geisser and Hildenbrand, 2006).

Furthermore, there was research on the coordination and collaboration in open source software development, which is most often conducted distributively. Gutwin et al. (2004) found that the team members of these projects often used techniques to support awareness. Commonly, tools like mailing lists or text based chats are applied (Gutwin et al., 2004).

2.3. Graphical User Interface Prototypes

A common method in requirements engineering to learn about a system being developed is prototyping. Prototypes of the system help to get a better understanding what the system should be able to do and how the functionality should be realized (Luqi and Royce, 1992). Prototypes exist in many different forms: from simple paper-based user interface prototypes (Snyder, 2003) to high fidelity and functional evolutionary prototypes, which enable stakeholders to experiment with the real software product (Gunaratne et al., 2004). Because of this variety, many different definitions of prototyping exist. Luqi and Royce (1992) define it in the following general way:

> *"Prototyping - the construction and analysis of an executable model that approximates a proposed system."* (Luqi and Royce, 1992, p.77).

Another definition by Lichter et al. (1994) is more detailed and contains an objective of prototyping:

> *"Prototyping is an approach based on an evolutionary view of software development, affecting the development process as a whole. Prototyping involves producing early working versions ('prototypes') of the future application system and experimenting with them"* (Lichter et al., 1994, p.826).

As said, there are many different kinds of prototypes and often these are low fidelity prototypes, which sketch out the (graphical) user interface but do not provide any functionality. These user interface prototypes are also called mockups as in the following definition by Rivero et al. (2010):

"A mockup is a sketch of a possible user interface (UI) of the application that helps to agree on broad aspects of the UI and can be easily created by any stakeholder" (Rivero et al., 2010, p.13).

Bäumer et al. (1996) differentiate between three different kinds of user interface prototyping: exploratory prototyping, experimental prototyping, and evolutionary prototyping. Exploratory prototyping is concerned with the understanding of the requirements. The needs of users and how the system can support these are discussed. In contrast, experimental prototyping deals with the technical implementation of the system. The objective is to learn if an implementation is suitable for the system. Finally, evolutionary prototyping deals with the adaption and extension of an existing system to changes and new requirements (Bäumer et al., 1996).

Bäumer et al. (1996) further classify the output of these kinds of interface prototyping into four classes of prototypes: presentation prototypes, functional prototypes, breadboards, and pilot systems. Presentation prototypes are intended to show how requirements are realized at the user interface. Presentation prototypes can be mockups without functionality. They are the result of exploratory prototyping. Functional prototypes go beyond the pure demonstration of the user interface and also implement parts of the functionality of the system. They are used in exploratory or experimental prototyping. Breadboards are not made for end user evaluation. Instead, their purpose is the evaluation of the architecture or other technical characteristics. Like functional prototypes, breadboards can also be used in experimental prototyping. Pilot

systems are prototypes that show a high level of maturity and are used in practical settings. Pilot systems are usually built during evolutionary prototyping
(Bäumer et al., 1996).

Prototyping in software development has many advantages and applications,
especially for requirements engineering (Gomaa and Scott, 1981). Prototypes
help users and developers to communicate as they provide a groundwork for
discussions (Lichter et al., 1994; Newman and Landay, 2000). They enable
users to experience a tangible representation of the system, which provides the
possibility to try out the influence of various design decisions (Ravid and Berry,
2000). As prototypes demonstrate possible solutions, unclear assumptions can
be clarified and unknown properties of the design can be discovered, which
enables changes to requirements early in the development process (Luqi and
Royce, 1992).

Prototypes facilitate the creation of ideas and the quality of a solution can
be assessed (Bäumer et al., 1996). When low fidelity prototypes, which only
sketch out the user interface and do not provide any functionality, are used, the
barrier for redesigning is low and many design variants can be tried out without
much effort. This enables many stakeholders – including users – to take part
in the design process, as the skills needed to sketch an interface are widespread
(Bowers and Pycock, 1994). These low fidelity sketches provide the possibility
to rapidly explore many ideas without the need to deal with dispensable details
(Lin et al., 2000).

Due to these characteristics, user interface prototyping is a popular technique during requirements elicitation (see Section 2.1.2.1), requirements analysis and negotiation (see Section 2.1.2.2), and requirements validation (see Section 2.1.2.4) (Ravid and Berry, 2000). Furthermore, it can also be used to try
out the impact of requirements changes during requirements management later
on in the process (Luqi and Royce, 1992). A particular application for pro-

totypes is usability engineering, where users can be observed while interacting
with the prototype (Walker et al., 2002).

Multiple empirical studies have shown the advantages of prototyping. Ricca
et al. (2010) conducted a study with 33 subjects, which assessed the understandability of functional requirements when they were complemented with screen
mockups. The results demonstrate that the understandability of the requirements improved significantly when they were supplemented with screen mockups. Furthermore, no additional effort was found (Ricca et al., 2010). A study
by Keil and Carmel (1995) examined customer-developer links in 31 different
projects, which were conducted in 17 companies. The links enable customers
and developers to exchange information. User interface prototyping was seen as
the customer-developer link with the highest effectiveness by project managers
(Keil and Carmel, 1995).

It can be distinguished between throwaway and evolutionary prototypes.
Throwaway prototypes are rough prototypes, which are created quickly without
many details in order to elicit new or validate existing requirements, and are
abandoned afterwards (Davis and Bersoff, 1991; Gomaa and Scott, 1981). At
first sight, throwaway prototypes seem to waste time and effort, as they are dis-
carded after use. But as code is often abandoned during development anyway,
because it was grounded on flawed requirements, it costs less to elicit correct
requirements and discard quickly created and cheap prototypes rather than
expensive code (Luqi and Royce, 1992). Thus, throwaway prototypes reduce
development costs, because the amount of changes during the implementation
of the software is reduced (Davis and Bersoff, 1991).

Furthermore, there are also risks involved with throwaway prototypes. Developers sometimes have difficulties to stop prototyping because creating and
changing prototypes is quick and involves little effort (Davis and Bersoff, 1991).
Furthermore, when a throwaway prototype also involves the implementation of

functionality, there is the risk that customers want developers to extend it until it is a production quality system. However, the prototype was never designed to become such a system and it is not possible to reach the level of quality and robustness needed for a production system (Davis and Bersoff, 1991).

Another kind of prototypes are evolutionary prototypes, which are designed to become production quality systems in the end. Quality and robustness is planned from the beginning. The prototypes are demonstrated in order to get customer feedback. This uncovers new or changes existing requirements. Hereupon, the prototypes are modified until they converge to a production quality system (Davis, 1992). Davis and Bersoff (1991) recommend that throwaway prototypes are used to build the parts of the system which lack a good understanding, whereas evolutionary prototypes should begin with the parts that are well understood and build upon this base (Davis and Bersoff, 1991).

Another classification of prototypes, which is found in literature, is the differentiation between low and high fidelity prototypes (Rudd et al., 1996). Low fidelity prototypes have restricted functionality and interaction capabilities. They are build to demonstrate concepts, design ideas and the user interface. The goal is to support communication and inform stakeholders, e.g., customers. Low fidelity prototypes are not intended to show the operation of the system or to test it (Rudd et al., 1996). Low fidelity prototypes are often created with low effort methods like sketching on whiteboards or paper, where users can easily be integrated (McCurdy et al., 2006; Sidhavatula and Wendt, 2007). These methods adopt some techniques from graphic design (Wong, 1992).

The advantages of low fidelity prototypes are that alternative ideas and concepts can be created rapidly with low effort. Furthermore, a common language for developers and customers is provided, which helps to create a mutual understanding of the system (Rudd et al., 1996). These prototypes are useful tools for requirements elicitation. Users often cannot express requirements in such way that they can be implemented by developers adequately. Low fidelity prototypes provide a basis for discussions and feedback (Rudd et al., 1996). Moreover low fidelity prototypes let stakeholders focus on the main concepts of the interface design and do not overwhelm them with low level details (Walker et al., 2002).

On the other hand, high fidelity prototypes are more detailed. They resemble the final system to a higher degree than low fidelity prototypes and are often created with similar methods than the final product (Walker et al., 2002). The prototypes span from detailed graphical representations of the user interface to functional and interactive emulations of the system (Memmel et al., 2007; Rudd et al., 1996). They can be used when clients demand a more realistic representation of the system and can help to convince the management (Newman and Landay, 2000; McCurdy et al., 2006). A disadvantage is the risk that the design space is analyzed less completely, because high fidelity prototypes a more difficult to change (Walker et al., 2002). Furthermore, it could be the case that they are simply to expensive to develop or that stakeholders get to high expectations when they see the prototypes (McCurdy et al., 2006).

Table 2.1 shows the advantages and disadvantages of low and high fidelity prototypes. The types of prototypes which are supported by this research are throwaway, low fidelity prototypes, as they can be created quickly and without a lot of effort. They are useful to try out a lot of different design ideas without overwhelming stakeholders with low level details.

2.4. Design Science Research

Design science is a research method that is based on a problem solving paradigm and is aimed to create innovative artifacts which solve real world problems (March and Smith, 1995; Hevner et al., 2004). It is founded on the sciences

Table 2.1.: Characteristics of Low and High Fidelity Prototypes (Rudd et al., 1996)

Type	Advantages	Disadvantages
Low fidelity prototype	Lower development cost	Limited error checking
	Evaluate multiple design concepts	Poor detailed specification to code to
	Useful communication device	Facilitator-driven
	Address screen layout issues	Limited utility after requirements established
	Useful for identifying market requirements	Limited usefulness for usability tests
	Proof-of-concept	Navigational and flow limitations
High fidelity prototype	Complete functionality	More expensive to develop
	Fully interactive	Time-consuming to create
	User-driven	Inefficient for proof-of-concept designs
	Clearly defines navigational scheme	Not effective for requirements gathering
	Use for exploration and test	
	Look and feel of final product	
	Serves as a living specification	
	Marketing and sales tool	

of the artificial by Simon (1996). Simon contrasts the sciences of the artificial with the sciences of the natural. It is to be distinguished from behavioral science, which is a problem understanding paradigm and seeks to create theories (Niehaves, 2007; Hevner et al., 2004). As the objective of this research is the creation of innovative artifacts to solve problems with requirements engineering, this research will follow the design science research method.

In order to achieve the goal of design science, different artifacts can be constructed. March and Smith (1995) identify four classes of artifacts: constructs, models, methods, and instantiations. Constructs provide vocabulary and symbols for the representation of problems and its solutions, whereas models use constructs to create abstractions and representations of the world (Hevner et al., 2004). Methods describe processes, practices and algorithms which deliver guidance to the solution of problems. Instantiations implement constructs, models and methods, show the feasibility of the solution, and provide the possibility to evaluate the appropriateness for the problem. This research contributes two artifacts, which address the problems of the early requirements engineering phase:

1. A *method* that supports knowledge transfer and sharing as well as communication and collaboration between stakeholders in globally distributed development scenarios for the requirements elicitation and analysis phase (see Section 4.1).

2. A *software tool* that acts as an instantiation and implements the method. This prototypical implementation shows the usefulness of the method and demonstrates its feasibility (see Section 4.2).

The creation of the artifacts developed in design science research should be informed by theories (Hevner et al., 2004; Markus et al., 2002; Walls et al., 1992). Theories could deliver valuable knowledge about the problem and its

Table 2.2.: Design Science Research Guidelines by Hevner et al. (2004)

Guideline	Description
Guideline 1: Design as an Artifact	Design science research must produce a viable artifact in the form of a construct, a model, a method, or an instantiation.
Guideline 2: Problem Relevance	The objective of design science research is to develop technology-based solutions to important and relevant business problems.
Guideline 3: Design Evaluation	The utility, quality, and efficacy of a design artifact must be rigorously demonstrated via well-executed evaluation methods.
Guideline 4: Research Contributions	Effective design science research must provide clear and verifiable contributions in the areas of the design artifact, design foundations, andor design methodologies.
Guideline 5: Research Rigor	Design science research relies upon the application of rigorous methods in both the construction and evaluation of the design artifact.
Guideline 6: Design as a Search Process	The search for an effective artifact requires utilizing available means to reach desired ends while satisfying laws in the problem environment.
Guideline 7: Communication of Research	Design science research must be presented effectively both to technology-oriented as well as management-oriented audiences.

causal mechanisms in order to constrain the solution space and derive design principles and implications, which guide the development of effective and efficient artifacts. This research draws on three theoretical concepts, which are presented in Chapter 3.

Hevner et al. (2004) suggest guidelines for high quality design science research (see Table 2.2). The guidelines should assure that a viable artifact is created, which solves a relevant problem. Furthermore, the utility of the artifact should be evaluated and a clear contribution to research should be made. Design science should follow a rigorous research method and should represent a search process in order to come up with a good solution. Finally, the results of the research process should be communicated adequately to the relevant audience (Hevner et al., 2004).

In order to demonstrate the utility of the artifact, it has to be evaluated appropriately (Pries-Heje et al., 2008). For this purpose, a suitable metric has to be used. According to Hevner et al. (2004), "IT artifacts can be evaluated in terms of functionality, completeness, consistency, accuracy, performance, reliability, usability, fit with the organization, and other relevant quality attributes" (Hevner et al., 2004, p.85). Furthermore, various evaluation methods can be used. These can be, for instance, observational (e.g., case studies), analytical (e.g., architecture analyses), experimental (e.g., controlled experiment), testing (e.g., functional testing), and descriptive (e.g., informed argument) methods (Hevner et al., 2004).

2.5. Related Research

This research deals with requirements engineering in distributed development projects. Thus, related to this research is work in the field of distributed requirements engineering. While there is a multitude of work for requirements engineering in co-located settings[3], there has been published less research regarding distributed requirements engineering.

Herlea and Greenberg (1998) used a groupware system, which provided tools for synchronous and asynchronous collaboration, such as notes, bulletin boards, brainstorming and voting tools, and chats. They adapted it for the requirements negotiation process. Lloyd et al. (2002) examined requirements elicitation techniques in distributed environments. They conducted an empirical study with six remote teams. The participants role-played as requirements engineers or

---

3 For an overview see, e.g., van Lamsweerde (2000); Nuseibeh and Easterbrook (2000); Cheng and Atlee (2007); Hull et al. (2010); Pohl (2010).

customers and used several techniques to elicit requirements, e.g., interviews, brainstorming, or questionnaires. The study shows that the participants were more effective when they used synchronous collaboration (Lloyd et al., 2002).

Damian and Zowghi (2003a) studied software development projects in two global organizations. They examined how stakeholders at various distributed locations specified requirements. The results of the study show that distributed requirements engineering exhibits many challenges. These challenges result from problems like cultural diversity, inadequate communication, knowledge management, and time differences Damian and Zowghi (2003a).

Hsieh (2006) examines the impact of culture on shared understanding of the requirements. They discuss several theoretical concepts and derive research questions for future research. Damian et al. (2008) examined how communication media affects the performance of distributed teams during requirements engineering. They analyzed six academic teams, which used asynchronous and synchronous media for communication. Their results show that the effectiveness of synchronous requirements negotiation sessions were higher when the participants performed asynchronous discussions about the requirements beforehand (Damian et al., 2008).

Geisser (2008) developed an integrated method for distributed requirements engineering, which supports requirements elicitation and analysis, requirements specification, requirements validation as well as requirements management. The method uses collaborative software tools to support the stakeholders. A wiki is used to elicit and specify requirements. For requirements analysis, a web-based prioritization tool was developed. Furthermore, a tracking tool is applied for requirements management. Compared to conventional document-based requirements engineering, Geisser (2008) shows in a controlled experiment that the method improved efficiency and the quality of the requirements.

The requirements engineering technique this work examines, is prototyping of graphical user interfaces. There is some existing research related to GUI prototyping (e.g., Bäumer et al. (1996); Keil and Carmel (1995); Landay and Myers (1995); Ricca et al. (2010)), but to the author's knowledge, there is no published work which examines GUI prototyping in distributed software projects.

An early work of Wong (1992) discusses the idea that developers can learn from graphic designers when creating user interfaces. Rough interface sketches focus discussions to general functional issues and enable quick turnaround times. Landay and Myers (1995) developed a software prototyping tool, which simulates the work with paper prototypes. It uses a graphic tablet for user input and recognizes gestures. Prototypes can be enhanced with annotations and simulate behavior via linking of screens. Landay and Myers (2001) report the results of an evaluation for the tool, which shows its effectiveness to communicate design ideas.

Keil and Carmel (1995) analyzed customer-developer links for 31 projects in 17 companies. The results show that user-interface prototyping was one of the most effective customer-developer link to improve the product. A study by Bäumer et al. (1996) showed similar results. They examined 19 industrial projects and conclude that prototyping was essential for the successful projects. Lin et al. (2000) created a prototyping tool for web designers. It is related to the tool of Landay and Myers (1995), but was extended with functionality for web design and a zoomable interface. They evaluated the tool with several experts and collected positive feedback. An extended version of the work was published in Newman et al. (2003).

Walker et al. (2002) conducted a study to examine the difference of low-fidelity and high-fidelity user interface prototypes for usability testing. They conclude that both low-fidelity and high-fidelity prototypes can be applied equally well for usability tests. Sidhavatula and Wendt (2007) discuss GUI prototypes as a way to involve users in the design process of software systems. They show how these prototypes can be beneficial and improve the design.

Ricca et al. (2007) conducted a study to examine the influence of GUI prototypes on the understandability of use cases. Their results show that the prototypes facilitate the understanding of the functional requirements. Furthermore, the effort for the stakeholders did not increase (Ricca et al., 2007). Rivero et al. (2010) developed an approach to create formal models from GUI prototypes. These models can then be used to generate code.

In conclusion, existing research showed that GUI prototyping can be an effective technique for software development. It improves understandability of requirements and facilitates communication. However, there is a lack of research on GUI prototyping in distributed software development projects. As distributed projects are more and more common today, this thesis intends to fill this gap. It examines the question how GUI prototypes can efficiently and effectively be applied in these projects and provides a method and tool for this purpose.

3. Theory-informed Design

This chapter is about the derivation of design implications from theory. Design science research requires that the design of artifacts is informed by theory
(Hevner et al., 2004; Markus et al., 2002; Walls et al., 1992). Thus, the next
section introduces theoretical concepts and derives design implications for the
artifacts. These theoretical works are the concept of boundary objects (see
Section 3.1.1), the Cognitive-Affective Model of Organizational Communication for Designing IT (see Section 3.1.2), and the Media Synchronicity Theory
(see Section 3.1.3). Furthermore, Section 3.2 summarizes the derived design
implications and Section 3.3 reports the results of a preliminary assessment of
those by industry experts. Finally, Section 3.4 evaluates and compares existing
prototyping tools. It is checked, if they fulfill the requirements of the design
implications.

3.1. Theoretical Concepts

3.1.1. Boundary Objects

As described above, globally distributed software development projects are char-
acterized by multiple stakeholders with different professional and cultural backgrounds, who are located at different sites around the globe. These stakeholders
have to communicate, transfer and share knowledge and coordinate their work
(Damian, 2007). This thesis aims to support the stakeholders' work in this difficult setting. Hence, a theoretical concept from sociology, which explains how

knowledge sharing and transfer and, thus, communication and coordination can be improved, is needed. The idea of *boundary objects*[1] is such a theoretical concept developed by Star and Griesemer (1989). It shows how people from different communities of practice can work together in an effective and efficient way.

A community of practice is a group of people who share the same interest or profession (Wenger, 1998). They work in the same domain or do similar work. People in these different communities of practice make use of an object as a means to communicate, get a shared understanding about their work and align their activities, even if they have different backgrounds, vocabulary, and knowledge. These objects are called boundary objects. Boundary objects facilitate communication, knowledge transfer and sharing across different communities. People from different communities can use these objects to facilitate communication and knowledge sharing because these objects are designed in such a way that everybody can understand the essential parts of the objects and interpret them in the same way. Beyond that, these objects also provide the possibilities for each community to use and interpret it for its benefit.

Boundary objects support an overlap of meaning but are also flexible enough so that each group can derive their own meanings (Barrett and Oborn, 2010; Star and Griesemer, 1989). Therefore, these objects help to create a common understanding of concepts like requirements between stakeholders. Carlile (2002) provides a categorization of different types of boundary objects. These are repositories, standardized forms, objects or models, and maps. The most useful of these are objects, models, and maps (Carlile, 2002). Objects and models are e.g. "sketches, assembly drawings, parts, prototype assemblies, mock-

---

1 Boundary objects have been used various times in the information systems literature. Examples are: Ackerman and Halverson (1999); Doolin and McLeod (2012); Levina and Vaast (2005); Pawlowski et al. (2000); Pawlowski and Robey (2004).

ups, and computer simulations" (Carlile, 2002, p.451). Star and Griesemer
(1989) describe boundary objects as the following:

"Boundary objects are objects which are both plastic enough to adapt
to local needs and the constraints of the several parties employing
them, yet robust enough to maintain a common identity across sites.
They are weakly structured in common use, and become strongly
structured in individual-site use" (Star and Griesemer, 1989, p.393).

The challenges of communication and knowledge transfer between stakeholders in global software development projects match well with the setting of the
different communities of practice described by the concept of boundary objects. Therefore, the usage of such objects should also be applicable to the
activities of requirements elicitation and analysis in such projects. Hence, a
usable boundary object, which facilitates knowledge transfer and communication between distributed stakeholders carrying out requirements elicitation and
analysis, needs to be found. The boundary object used must show the characteristics described above in the definition of Star and Griesemer (1989).

On the one hand, it must be robust enough to serve as an object which can be
used as a mediator. Everyone in the project needs to understand the semantics
of the objects so that communication about it is possible. It should provide a
shared meaning, which means the concepts that are embodied in the object are
interpreted by all stakeholders in a similar way. Thus, a shared mental model[2]
and common understanding of these concepts is facilitated. On the other hand,
it must be flexible and plastic enough to serve the specific needs of individual
stakeholders, so that stakeholders can use the objects for their specific tasks
which they have to accomplish. Furthermore, they need a sufficient degree

---

2 A mental model is a representation of the outside world in the mind of a person.

of flexibility for manipulation to ensure that tacit knowledge about a specific problem can be externalized by the stakeholders and represented in the object.

In order to identify such an adequate boundary object for the usage in the scenario outlined above, literature about requirements elicitation and analysis techniques (e.g., brainstorming, interviews, business process modeling, observation, and graphical user interface prototyping, Zowghi and Coulin, 2005) was reviewed. The artifacts used by the techniques were evaluated. It was assessed if they show the characteristics of suitable boundary objects. After this review GUI prototyping was identified as a promising technique (Bäumer et al., 1996), because the prototypes show the needed boundary object characteristics that have been described above. GUI prototypes are early representations of the part of the system that is visible by the user (see Section 2.3).

These prototypes, also known as mockups or wire frames, are very popular in software development projects. In particular, they are very popular in projects that follow an agile software development methodology, which is one of the most promising software development methodologies in the recent years (Lee and Xia, 2010). The prototypes help to visualize the system, support the stakeholders of the system to get a clearer picture of their requirements, and serve as a tool to quickly try out various ideas and functionalities. They facilitate a common understanding of the requirements of a system, both on the developer and the user side, and improve the usability of the product (Arnowitz et al., 2007). Ricca et al. (2010) examined the effectiveness of GUI prototypes in requirements engineering and discovered significant improvements regarding the understandability of requirements when prototypes were used. Moreover, Keil and Carmel (1995) analyzed customer-developer links for 31 projects in 17 companies. They showed that user-interface prototyping was one of the most effective customer-developer link to improve the product.

GUI prototypes exist on a multitude of sophistication levels: from simple paper-based sketches to dynamic functional graphical user interfaces created with heavy weighted interface creation applications (Rudd et al., 1996). Especially, in the very first phase of the development and in agile projects, often simple, paper-based prototypes are used in order to visualize and try out ideas quickly (Chamberlain et al., 2006). The meaning of the concepts they represent is easily shared by all stakeholders. This supports a common understanding of the requirements. In addition, the prototypes can be used by different stakeholders in their specific ways. E.g., software end users can use the prototypes to think about the tasks they need to execute during their work or evaluate the usability of the software product. Software developers can use the prototypes as a first specification of requirements on a more technical level, such as the different types of data the application needs as input.

Thus, GUI prototypes show the characteristics of boundary objects as defined by Star and Griesemer (1989). They are at the same time both plastic and robust enough and support knowledge transfer and a common understanding of requirements because all stakeholders understand the meaning of the prototypes. Especially, non-technical stakeholders do not have to learn a special syntax and semantics of other notations for models in software development, such as UML diagrams. It can be concluded that GUI prototypes can serve as boundary objects in requirements engineering and support the activities of requirements elicitation and analysis (cp. Brandt, 2007; Gunaratne et al., 2004).

In globally distributed software development projects, different stakeholders are located at different sites around the globe. Hence, in such scenarios, knowledge sharing and transfer is not only hindered by different people working together but also by challenges of spacial and temporal distance and cultural and language differences. Also in such settings, boundary objects can provide support (Hildreth et al., 2000), but there must be means to use these objects over distances. To enable this usage, methods and tools have to be developed. This is an objective of this thesis.

Furthermore, the method and tool must support the characteristics of GUI prototypes as boundary objects. This means at the same time flexibility and structure must be stimulated in order to be plastic and robust. Structure for GUI prototypes can be provided if common and well-known user interface elements, so-called widgets (e.g., buttons, menus, dialog boxes), are used. These elements can be easily understood by all stakeholders. Thus, a design implication for the method and tool is that such GUI widgets should be supported.

Furthermore, flexibility can be provided when users are given the possibility to create freehand sketches. When users can freely sketch and create any kind of graphical object, the prototypes can be plastic enough for local needs. For instance, the client in a software development project could need custom icons, which have special meaning for his business process. This can also stimulate creativity. Hence, another design implication for the method and tool is the possibility to create such freehand sketches.

In this section, the basic theoretical concept of boundary objects, which supports collaboration of different communities of practice, was introduced. Furthermore, GUI prototypes as appropriate boundary objects for requirements elicitation and analysis activities were identified and two design implications for the method and tool were derived. In the next sections two theories from the field of information systems are used to derive further design implications.

3.1.2. Cognitive-Affective Model of Organizational Communication for Designing IT

As outlined in the previous section, a method and tool is needed that enable different stakeholders to use GUI prototypes as boundary objects collaboratively over distance. This collaboration of the stakeholders needs sophisticated communication processes, which have to be supported by the method and tool. Therefore, a theoretical model of organizational communication was selected to inform and guide the design of the new method and tool. This theoretical model is the Cognitive-Affective Model of Organizational Communication for Designing IT by Te'eni (2001). It examines the usage of communication media taking into account different communication situations and goals. The model relates communication inputs (e.g., task characteristics and sender-receiver distance) with the communication process (communication goals, strategies, media and message forms). It explains which communication process is appropriate to achieve communication impact (e.g. mutual understanding) given certain communication inputs.

The model of Te'eni (2001) uses the concept of *cognitive complexity* of communication. Cognitive complexity rises when information exchange is intense, many communicators with a variety of views are involved, or the representation of information and its use are incompatible. High intensity of information exchange and a variety of views lead to a higher probability that information is misunderstood or understood in a different context. When the representation of information and its use are incompatible, a translation is needed, which is more costly and error-prone. Activities which involve a high degree of cognitive complexity are, e.g., non-routine situations, which need a complex exchange of perspectives (Te'eni, 2001).

Requirements elicitation and analysis and its support with the help of collaborative distributed GUI prototyping can involve such kind of activities. Often, there are a variety of different stakeholders with a multitude of views involved in the requirements elicitation and analysis activities (Sharp et al., 1999; Decker et al., 2007; Nuseibeh et al., 1994). Clients, requirements analysts, architects, developers, and project managers all have different backgrounds, goals and perspectives. In many cases, the activities are also inherently non-routine as each global software development project is unique. It involves different stakeholders, who perform diverse roles at different locations and have a unique set of tasks, goals and requirements (Majchrzak et al., 2005). Due to this, the new method and tool must support activities which show a high cognitive complexity.

When cognitive complexity is high, the model of Te'eni (2001) proposes that *contextualization* is required to mitigate the risk of misunderstandings. Contextualization provides explicit context to the messages transferred in the communication process. The context contains, e.g., related information or information about the participants of the communication process (Te'eni, 2001). The related information helps to deepen the understanding of the messages and reduce the chances for misinterpretations. Majchrzak et al. (2005) conducted a study with 263 subjects in 54 distributed teams. They found a positive relationship between contextualization and development of collaboration know-how when the individuals performed non-routine work.

However, providing contextual information in distributed projects is difficult. Contextual information, which is often provided implicitly when working in face-to-face settings, has to be added explicitly in distributed projects. It is even more important in these settings, as the likelihood of misunderstandings is higher than in face-to-face teams as stakeholders often have different cultural and professional backgrounds (Katz and Te'eni, 2007). In order to provide contextual information when creating GUI prototypes distributedly, several design implications can be derived:

- Stakeholders must be able to link GUI prototypes to other related artifacts. The other artifacts provide information related to the information provided by the prototypes. This could be, e.g., more detailed information about the requirements which are illustrated by the prototypes, or information about related requirements. The artifacts linked to the prototypes can be artifacts created in requirements engineering activities, like textual requirements specifications or artifacts created in other development phases, like architectural design documents or code. The links can not only connect other artifacts with whole GUI prototypes, but also individual elements of the prototypes to provide more specificity.

- Stakeholders must have the possibility to link prototypes or elements of the prototypes with other prototypes or its elements. This provides context about the integration of the functionality provided by a certain view of the GUI with other views. Furthermore, it could provide context about the processes which have to be followed to accomplish the tasks in certain use cases.

- The method must link the actions and changes when the prototypes are edited with the stakeholders executing these actions and changes. Thus, context is provided about the individuals who collaborate on the prototypes. Stakeholders can trace what a person contributed, which helps to understand and interpret the contributions in a better way. Furthermore, it helps participants who do not take part in the creation of the prototypes to reconstruct the creation process in later development phases and provides them with the information to contact these stakeholders in case of ambiguity.

3.1.3. Media Synchronicity Theory

As the method and tool must use a communication medium for the information exchange between the stakeholders, a second theory that examines the choice of communication media was selected. The Media Synchronicity Theory by Dennis et al. (2008) informs about the suitability of media synchronicity dependent on the characteristics of the communication processes. In the case of this work, the communication processes are essential for the stakeholders' collaboration on the GUI prototypes. A study by Niinimäki et al. (2010) examined 12 globally distributed software development projects on communication tool choices. Their results are supported by the Media Synchronicity Theory (Niinimäki et al., 2010).

The Media Synchronicity Theory describes two primary communication processes: conveyance and convergence. Conveyance processes transmit a variety of new and detailed information. The receiver of the new information uses it for the creation or update of a mental model. The amount of information transmitted can potentially be high and the receiver often needs time to process it. In contrast, during convergence processes, individuals discuss their preprocessed information and their interpretation. The goal of convergence is to get a common understanding of the meaning of the information (Dennis and Valacich, 1999; Dennis et al., 2008).

Media Synchronicity Theory proposes that convergence processes benefit from highly synchronous media, because communication participants have the need to quickly transfer and process information in smaller amounts. For conveyance processes, on the other hand, media with lower level of synchronicity is beneficial, because large amounts of detailed information have to be transferred and processed, which needs time. Furthermore, Media Synchronicity Theory concludes that most tasks in practice (e.g., decision-making) will need both conveyance and convergence processes. Therefore, the use of multiple media, asynchronous and synchronous, is favorable (Dennis et al., 2008).

The activities carried out in requirements elicitation and analysis are such conveyance and convergence processes. A lot of detailed and new information about requirements has to be transferred (e.g., from users to developers). This implies conveyance processes, which are best supported by media with a low degree of synchronicity. Additionally, stakeholders have to agree on the meaning of these requirements to get a common understanding and discuss and negotiate them. This is a difficult task because of the different backgrounds of the stakeholders and the different goals they have (Nuseibeh and Easterbrook, 2000). Thus, for this processes, highly synchronous media should be used according to Media Synchronicity Theory.

The need for asynchronous and synchronous media for communication in requirements engineering is also supported in a study by Damian et al. (2008). It shows evidence that synchronous requirements negotiation meetings are more effective when the requirements are discussed asynchronously beforehand, which is contrary to the traditional belief that synchronous communication is the most effective means for requirements negotiation. Damian et al. (2008) argue that there is a constant interplay between the the reduction of uncertainties and ambiguities. Collecting and processing information reduces uncertainties. After this, negotiating and resolving conflicts takes place, which reduces ambiguities in the understanding of the requirements. These processes repeat by means of several iterations of asynchronous work and synchronous meetings (Damian et al., 2008).

As the method and tool developed in this work should support the collaboration on GUI prototypes between distributed stakeholders, communication media have to be used to enable the information transfer between the different locations. Also, in this case, conveyance and convergence processes are needed to support efficient and effective knowledge sharing and collaboration. For instance, a conveyance process could be the transfer of a detailed draft of functionality via a GUI prototype from a developer to the client. An example for a convergence process is the negotiation about implications and importance of requirements embodied in a GUI prototype. Because of this, the method and tool should offer both media with low and high synchronicity to support the distributed collaboration on requirements.

Also Dennis et al. (2008) conclude that for a certain task, a combination of media could be beneficial. They provide the example of adding a whiteboard to a face-to-face convergence process. The combination of both media should be more efficient and effective, because the whiteboard adds its capability to provide reprocessability of information to the synchronicity of face-to-face communication (Dennis et al., 2008).

Taking these considerations into account, the propositions of the Media Synchronicity Theory lead to two design implications for the method and tool developed in this thesis:

- *Asynchronous* work on GUI prototypes must be supported. Stakeholders should be able to create and edit prototypes individually and asynchronously. The results of these edits must be viewable for all further stakeholders afterwards. Additionally, the individual editing steps must be traceable, so that everybody can understand who did what and when.

- *Synchronous* work must be supported. Stakeholders must be able to collaborate on the GUI prototypes in real-time. All editing steps have to be replicated instantly on all locations. In addition, stakeholders should be able to discuss the prototypes via a synchronous medium.

3.2. Design Implications

This section summarizes the design implications derived from the theoretical concepts in the previous sections. Table 3.1 lists the design implications for the method and tool.

The first two implications have been derived from the theoretical concept of boundary objects, which was introduced in Section 3.1.1. As explained in that section, the method and tool should support templates for GUI widgets.

Table 3.1.: Summary of the Design Implications

Design implication	Derived from
Template GUI widgets	Boundary objects (Star and Griesemer, 1989)
Freehand sketches	Boundary objects (Star and Griesemer, 1989)
Asynchronous collaboration	Media Synchronicity Theory (Dennis et al., 2008)
Synchronous collaboration	Media Synchronicity Theory (Dennis et al., 2008)
Linking of prototypes with other artifacts and stakeholders	Cognitive-Affective Model of Organizational Communication for Designing IT (Te'eni, 2001)

These templates are, e.g., buttons, menus, or other controls and UI elements, which can be used in the prototypes without further effort. The second design implication is the ability to create freehand sketches. This enables stakeholders to create arbitrary task-specific graphical elements and sketch out ideas quickly as on paper or whiteboards.

The design implications of asynchronous and synchronous collaboration in Table 3.1 result from the Media Synchronicity Theory (see Section 3.1.3). Stakeholders should be able to work synchronously or asynchronously depending on the needs of their current communication process. The Cognitive-Affective Model by Te'eni (2001) also contributes a design implication, namely the linking of the prototypes with other prototypes, artifacts, or stakeholders. These links provide contextual information, which is crucial for communication processes of high cognitive complexity that are common in requirements engineering.

3.3. Preliminary Evaluation

As a preliminary check of the derived design implications, three experts from the software industry have been interviewed to examine if the implications are valid. The experts work at different international software companies with 50 to several 1000 employees. Expert A is a product owner at a company, which develops media streaming software at various locations in Germany and Eastern Europe. Expert B works as a project manager at a software company, which develops custom made business software and websites at locations in Germany and Eastern Europe. Expert C is a Scrum Master[3] at an enterprise software company, which has development centers worldwide. All experts had several years of experience in the field of software development.

The experts were asked several questions regarding their software development process and the stakeholders they have to deal with. In particular, they were asked if they use GUI prototypes and how they create them.

Expert A mentioned the importance of the ability to be flexible when sketching out prototypes. When collaborating on prototypes in distributed settings, the characteristics of a whiteboard should be maintained:

> *"To support flexible freehand drawing also makes a lot of sense when working distributedly on mockups as a substitution for conventional whiteboard functionality."* – Expert A.

This supports the design implication freehand sketches. This implication is also supported by expert B, who pointed out the requirement of being able to create user-specific elements, which needs flexible drawing tools:

> *"But what can also be the case is that you need to design a customized element [...]. That you can define your own elements. And with the drawing say: these are our buttons and they are used for this and that. That would mean an extension of the default elements. That would be great."* – Expert B.

---

3 Scrum is an agile development methodology (see Schwaber, 2004).

While talking about his work process, expert B mentioned the advantages a synchronous session for editing prototypes would have:

"When I have a meeting with the client, I sometimes need deeper knowledge how something can be realized. This is knowledge that the development has. We could go online and invite a developer to the meeting, sketch something quickly and both sides could work with that, give feedback, and add something." – Expert B.

Also, linking of prototypes to requirements specification documents was found helpful by the expert:

"It would be good if I would have the button [in the prototype] and when I click on the button and would have the link to the page, e.g., the wiki, where there is the definition [of its function]: print invoice. Or maybe the process. [...] Maybe, where do I have to save it." – Expert B.

This design implication was also supported by the following statement of expert A:

"If there is a tool that provides this possibility of linking various tools, files, websites, and documents so that they make sense semantically, it is definitely an important feature. We definitely have this problem. For instance, we have a wiki, and a tracking tool, and emails and so on and all runs into development. All this belongs to the process. But of course, it is tremendously difficult to follow several paths afterwards, because we work with different tools for different purposes. That's because I think that it is a very important and helpful feature." – Expert B.

The expert interviews further revealed another design implication which has not been derived from the theories. The experts stated that a tool for distributed GUI prototyping must be simple to use and should not require any installation procedures. A statement from expert B illustrates this:

"Such a tool should be web-based and simple. It should not be overloaded. It should deliver the basics." – Expert B.

Thus, the design implication is that the tool should be lightweight like a web application, which runs on any web browser and does not have to be installed. The advantage of this is that a greater range of project stakeholders can be integrated into the collaboration process. Also, clients could use the tool without a lot of effort. The problem that clients often cannot install software on their systems is avoided.

3.4. Existing Tools

In order to check, if existing tools meet the requirements, which are determined by the design implications of Section 3.2, a literature and market research was conducted via standard internet search engines. After searching with combinations of the keywords `prototyping`, `prototype`, `mockup`, `GUI`, `graphical user interface`, and `tool`, a list of academic and commercial tools was created. This list is shown in Table 3.2. The websites of the tools were thoroughly examined and the tools were given a trial as far as possible.

It was checked, if the tools of Table 3.2 support the discussed design implications. The results of this evaluation are shown in Table 3.3. The first design implication, the support for template GUI widgets, is support by almost all tools, except DENIM. DENIM is an academic prototype (see Lin et al., 2000; Newman et al., 2003) and supports only freehand sketching. It is build around

Table 3.2.: Existing Tools

Tool	Website	Type
Axure	`http://www.axure.com` (accessed 15/02/2009)	commercial
Balsamiq	`http://www.balsamiq.com` (accessed 15/02/2009)	commercial
DesignerVista	`http://www.designervista.com` (accessed 15/02/2009)	commercial
DENIM	`http://dub.washington.edu:2007/denim` (accessed 15/02/2009)	academic
GUI Design Studio	`http://www.carettasoftware.com` (accessed 15/02/2009)	commercial
iPlotz	`http://iplotz.com` (accessed 16/02/2009)	commercial
Justinmind Prototyper	`http://www.justinmind.com` (accessed 16/02/2009)	commercial
MockupScreens	`http://www.mockupscreens.com` (accessed 16/02/2009)	commercial
OverSite	`http://taubler.com/oversite` (accessed 18/02/2009)	commercial
Pencil	`http://www.evolus.vn/Pencil/Home.html` (accessed 18/02/2009)	commercial
ProtoShare	`http://www.ProtoShare.com` (accessed 18/02/2009)	commercial
Screen Architect	`http://screenarchitect.com` (accessed 18/02/2009)	commercial
Serena Prototype Composer	`http://www.serena.com` (accessed 18/02/2009)	commercial
WireframeSketcher	`http://wireframesketcher.com` (accessed 18/02/2009)	commercial

Table 3.3.: Characteristics of Existing Tools

Tool	Template GUI widgets	Freehand sketches	Asynchronous collaboration	Synchronous collaboration	Linking	Lightweight
Axure	✓		✓			
Balsamiq	✓				✓	
DesignerVista	✓					
DENIM		✓				
GUI Design Studio	✓					
iPlotz	✓				✓	✓
Justinmind Prototyper	✓					
MockupScreens	✓					
OverSite	✓					
Pencil	✓					
ProtoShare	✓		✓			✓
Screen Architect	✓				✓	
Serena PrototypeComposer	✓				✓	
WireframeSketcher	✓					

the idea to simulate the work previously done by paper or whiteboards. Furthermore, it is also the only tool which supports freehand sketches. The other tools offer a variety of predefined GUI widgets and allow the user to build prototypes with these building blocks. They do not enable the users to flexibly sketch their own elements.

Asynchronous collaboration is only supported by Axure and ProtoShare, and synchronous collaboration is not supported by any of the tools. Only few of the tools support links between prototypes or links to other artifacts. These are Balsamiq, Screen Architect, and Serena Prototype Composer. Moreover, the design implication derived from the expert interviews which requires a lightweight and web-based tool is supported by two tools: iPlotz and ProtoShare. As it can be seen by these results, no existing tool supports *all* of the required design implications. Thus, there is a need for a new tool, which is developed for this thesis.

4. Designed Artifacts

4.1. A Method for Distributed GUI Prototyping

The previous sections have shown why requirements engineering should benefit from GUI prototypes and that there is a need for a method for GUI prototyping in distributed software development projects. This method has to be supported by a tool which enables the distributed collaboration on the prototypes. Furthermore, theoretical concepts have been introduced and design implications for such a method and tool have been derived from those. In the following, the method based on these design implication is introduced. A software engineering method is an approach, which describes more or less precisely a way to systematically solve a software development problem (Heinrich et al., 2011). Thus, the next sections describe the way to solve the collaboration problems for distributed GUI prototyping. First, a conceptual overview of the new method is provided and its steps are depicted. After this, two example scenarios are presented.

4.1.1. Conceptual Overview of the Method

The method assumes that stakeholders are located at different places and collaborate on the GUI prototype with the help of a lightweight, browser-based tool. In this sense, lightweight means that no software application has to be downloaded and installed manually and the tool is easy to use. Furthermore, no browser plug-in is needed as the technology platform on the client side is standard HTML[1] and JavaScript. This design is based on the implications described in the previous Section 3.2. Stakeholders can create, edit and delete graphical elements, which are the building blocks for the GUI prototypes. These graphical elements can be freehand sketches to enable quick and flexible creation and visualization of design ideas. This enables stakeholders to use the tool with a high degree of flexibility and stimulates creativity. These sketches are also useful for synchronous discussions and negotiation sessions, because they are easy to create and flexible in their use. This leads to a quick exchange of information. Sketches can also be used for various types of annotations during these sessions.

Additionally, more structured graphical elements are available. These elements are based on template elements of typical GUI widgets used in software applications. They can be used to create more structured and formal prototypes and complement the freehand drawing tools. The template elements are in particular useful to create prototypes, which can be used as a detailed requirements specification. In contrast, the freehand sketches are more likely used at the very first step of the requirements and idea elicitation phase.

Stakeholders use the lightweight tool to either work in an asynchronous or synchronous mode. Asynchronous work is better suited for conveyance processes as outlined in Section 3.1.3. Convergence processes, on the other hand, benefit from synchronous work. When working asynchronously, stakeholders use the tool to create and edit the prototypes at different times. Each change, i.e., each graphical element edited, is being tracked by the tool. A history is available that shows which person changed which element at a certain point of time. Thus, everybody can trace the changes the other stakeholders made. This is important to provide context about the changes, can be helpful for dis-

---

1 HTML stands for Hypertext Markup Language and is a markup language for the structure of web pages.

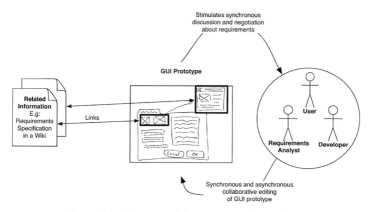

Figure 4.1.: Conceptual Overview of the Method

cussions, and provides stakeholders the possibility to contact the right person, if they need more information about a requirement or its rationale later in the process.

When stakeholders work synchronously on prototypes, the tool instantly replicates all changes made by a certain stakeholder in the browsers of the other stakeholders. Hence, everyone is always able to view the same state of the prototype. Stakeholders can immediately see the actions the other stakeholders take and react on them. Furthermore, stakeholders can use text, audio, or video-based chat tools to communicate and discuss while working on the prototype at the same time. Another possibility to use the tool synchronously is that one stakeholder (possibly a developer) just shows a prototype to another stakeholder (possibly a user), and both discuss it. To support this, the elements selected by the stakeholders are highlighted and the name of the person selecting it is shown next to it. Thus, everybody can see the elements currently discussed.

As outlined, a mixture of both asynchronous and synchronous collaboration is most efficient and effective. Stakeholders can work asynchronously, edit prototypes, and after that meet for a synchronous discussion session. The prototypes stimulate discussions and negotiations about requirements during this session. Furthermore, possible changes, which are discussed, can be integrated instantly by all stakeholders and are viewable by everyone so that immediate feedback is possible (see Figure 4.1).

In Section 3.1.2, it was explained that providing context is important for complex tasks like requirements elicitation and analysis. Stakeholders can provide this context for the prototypes or its elements using linking functionality. They can select elements or the whole prototype and add links to related artifacts such as, e.g., design documents, textual specifications, code, or any other artifact which provides related and possibly useful information. These artifacts can be stored in a variety of systems, e.g., document management systems, collaborative software development platforms, wikis, file servers, and source code management systems. To enable this flexibility, the links to the artifacts are based on simple HTTP[2] URLs[3]. Thus, any artifact which can be addressed with a URL can be linked.

It is possible for the stakeholders to trace these artifacts by following the link in the browser-based application. By following the link, the browser can open a new web page, e.g., a wiki page or a web-based view of a source code file. In addition to that, the links should be bidirectional, as indicated by the double-headed arrows in Figure 4.1. That means that every prototype and its elements provide a URL, which can be used in related artifacts to link back to the prototype or to a specific element of the prototype. Thus, stakeholders are able to access additional information embodied in prototypes when they work on the other artifacts. For instance, a developer who adds a change to a code

---

2 Hypertext Transfer Protocol (HTTP)
3 Uniform Resource Locator (URL)

file could make sure that it is still consistent with the requirements outlined in the related prototype.

In general, the links between the prototypes and other artifacts enable traceability throughout the project in two directions. From requirements and its rationals embedded in GUI prototypes to artifacts used later in the process, like design documents and code. The other way around is also possible. Furthermore, as all changes of the prototypes are tracked, traceability between different versions of the prototypes and between prototypes and responsible stakeholders is enabled. All these possibilities to access additional information provide context about related artifacts, why a specific design decision was made, and who was involved in this decision.

4.1.2. Steps of the Method

The prototyping tool can be applied in a variety of situations and cases. Two example scenarios are presented in the following section. As every project is different, there is no one-size-fits-all process model. Nevertheless, several general steps for the collaboration on the prototypes can be defined, which can be applied flexibly and iteratively in a development project:

1. *Collecting ideas*: Stakeholders meet via a video conference and use the GUI prototyping tool to quickly sketch out screens and rough ideas. The tool is used in cooperation with a wiki, where requirements are collected and described shortly in textual form. These requirements can be linked with the sketches in the prototyping tool. This scenario corresponds to work with paper or whiteboards in a co-located scenario. The tool supports the work with functionalities to draw graphical primitives like rectangles or polygons, but the most important feature is the freehand drawing tool. An enhancement in comparison to the work with paper or

physical whiteboards are the possibilities to cut, copy and paste, resize and stretch, and move parts of the sketch.

2. *Refining and enhancing*: The product owner uses the rough sketches as a draft and creates more elaborated prototypes. The tool supports this with graphical template widgets like dialog windows or menus. The widgets can either be inserted into the drawing surface next to the rough sketches or on new surfaces via drag and drop. To adapt the widgets to the needs of the project, they can be resized and text captions can be changed. During this scenario, the product owner builds upon the ideas of the workshop, refines them with his own requirements or requirements from different other sources he collected. In project teams, with more than one person having the responsibility to collect the requirements, this step can be repeated asynchronously.

3. *Presenting and negotiating*: The project manager and client stakeholders meet via a video conference. The project manager presents the prototypes which she created to the client stakeholders and shows them various use cases via clicking through different screens. This enables the transfer of knowledge and ideas about the system to be developed. The participants negotiate the different requirements by the means of the prototypes. This negotiation process helps to build a shared mental model of the requirements. If changes are requested, everybody can incorporate these directly into the prototypes. Thus, changes can be worked out and explained efficiently, as they do not have to be explained orally or in text form in the first place and then be implemented by another person.

4. *Tracing requirements during implementation*: When developers implement a requirement, they start with a textual specification. In agile projects this is often a user story, which they take from the backlog. This requirements specification can be linked to GUI prototypes in the pro-

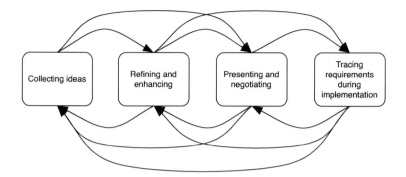

Figure 4.2.: Steps of the Method

totyping tool, so the developers can easily find graphical representations for the textual specification. This provides further insights about the intended functionality of the system. If necessary, they can further trace back from the prototypes to the first sketches and view the evolvement of the ideas as all changes are tracked and can be replayed by the tool. This is likely to improve the developers' understanding of the intentions of the stakeholders who brought up the requirement. If needed, they can also contact the respective persons directly as the tool tracks which user created or changed an element in the prototype.

Figure 4.2 shows these steps. It can be seen that the steps can applied flexibly and iteratively.

4.1.3. Example Scenarios

As the method which is proposed in this work can be used in many different software development processes and settings (e.g., waterfall-like processes, agile processes, custom software, standard software), two example usage scenarios how the method could be applied are outlined in the following.

4.1.3.1. Waterfall-like Process

The first scenario is a customer-specific Customer Relationship Management
(CRM) solution for a small and specialized financial service provider. The
client is located in Frankfurt, Germany. One project manager and three key
user representatives are involved in the project. The software development
company is located in Bangalore, India, employing a team of 10 developers, one
requirements engineer, one software architect, and one project manager. The
project is expected to last 1.5 years. The team follows a waterfall-like software
development process as described by Royce (1970).

The first step in the project is a face-to-face meeting in Germany with the
representatives from the customer, the requirements engineer, the software architect, and the project manager from the development company. This first
meeting ensures a certain level of trust between the stakeholders (Damian and
Zowghi, 2003a,b). During this first meeting, the overall vision of the software
application and first high level requirements are elicited and discussed. After
that, the project manager from the development company and the requirements
engineer in India, together, use the GUI prototyping tool to develop a first GUI
concept for the application. The architect regularly reviews the concept and
creates comments concerning software architecture issues in the tool.

When the first GUI concept draft is ready for presentation, customer representatives in Germany can review the concept asynchronously with the help
of the prototyping tool. After that, a synchronous telephone conference with
the customer representatives is arranged. During this conference, the tool is
used for the presentation of the GUI concept and the discussion of the requirements pictured by the prototypes. Developer company representatives can show
workflows of use cases by clicking on elements in the prototypes which link to
different views of the GUI. Customer representatives can remotely follow the

explanations, because they can see which elements are selected by the respective stakeholders in real time. Further changes, which emerge from the discussion, can directly be incorporated into the prototypes.

After the meeting, the requirements engineer creates textual requirements specifications in a wiki and links these with the prototypes. Customer representatives can review these specifications and the links to the prototypes asynchronously and comment on them in the wiki or the prototyping tool. The requirements engineer uses the comments to change the specification accordingly. If needed, a further telephone conference for reviewing and discussing the prototype and the requirements can be arranged. When the specification is final, the project continuous with the design, coding, and testing phases, which are conducted sequentially. After the application is tested and all issues are fixed, it is presented to the customer. In the design, development, and testing phases architects, developers, and testers can use the prototypes to make sure that they understood the requirements correctly and, if needed, get more information from the stakeholders responsible for creating the prototypes.

4.1.3.2. Agile Development

The first usage scenario example for the method was a custom-made software developed by a distributed team in a waterfall-like process. The second example shows that the method can also be used in agile development projects, which have become increasingly popular in recent years (Lee and Xia, 2010). In this example, a small software company develops a new release for their project management suite. The product can be classified as a standard Software-as-a-Service (SaaS)[4] product. The overall goals of this to be developed release

---

4 In the Software-as-a-Service model, the software is not installed at the clients site. Instead, the client subscribes to a software service which runs at data centers of the vendor and often accesses the software with a web browser (Sääksjärvi et al., 2005; Choudhary, 2007; Stuckenberg and Heinzl, 2010).

are new time-tracking functionalities and improvements in the usability of the application.

The team follows the agile method Scrum (Schwaber, 2004) as the development process, which subdivides the process into small iterations, so called sprints. The team expects a development time of four sprints of two weeks each. The company in this scenario is of small size but contracts people from different locations. The team consists of the product owner, scrum master, and three developers, who are located in Zurich, Switzerland. In addition, four freelance developers, who are located in Budapest, Hungary, are involved in the team. The stakeholders in the team know each other very well since they worked together for the previous five releases of the product. Thus, it is decided to start the distributed development without a face-to-face meeting.

As Scrum is an iterative development approach, requirements engineering is done throughout the whole development process, increasingly at the beginning of each sprint, because feedback from earlier sprints is essential for further development and requirements changes are embraced. At the beginning of the project a product backlog must be created. The product backlog is a prioritized list of all requirements which are to be implemented for the release. Before each sprint the developers pick the requirements they commit to implement in the current sprint. To create the product backlog, requirements have to be elicited. The product owner leads the elicitation in close collaboration with the development team.

For the elicitation, the prototyping tool can be used during a virtual one day planning meeting. All team members from Switzerland and Hungary communicate via a telephone conference and discuss the requirements for the release. The product owner leads the discussion. The prototyping tool is used during the meeting to visualize GUI design ideas and stimulate the discussion. Everybody can contribute to the prototypes and comment on them. Furthermore, notes for short user stories[5] are created in a wiki and linked with related prototypes.

After the meeting, the product owner consolidates, refines, and prioritizes the requirements represented by the user stories and the prototypes. In addition, the product owner transfers the user stories from the wiki into a web-based tracking system for the Scrum method. The entries in the tracking system are now the product backlog. These backlog entries are also linked to the respective prototypes. All stakeholders in the project can review the backlog and the prototypes, comment on them, or change them asynchronously at any time in the project. Changes are always tracked so that it is always clear who changed what and changes can be undone at any time.

Developers choose a certain set of backlog items from the top of the backlog to implement them in the next sprint. During the sprints, the prototypes, which are linked to a backlog item, provide valuable information to the developer who is responsible for the implementation of the backlog item. The developer can review the prototypes, their history of changes, their comments and get a better mental model of the requirements. If there are uncertainties or ambiguities, the developers can use the prototype as a boundary object in discussions with other team members.

4.2. A Tool for Distributed GUI Prototyping

To use the method that has been described in the previous sections, a tool is necessary. As shown in Section 3.4, no existing tool supports *all* of the required design implications. Hence, there is a need for a new tool. This tool is

---

5 A user story describes with a few short sentences a software requirement. It is written in everyday language.

described in the following sections. It has been named *ProtoColl*, which stands for *proto*typing *coll*aboratively.

4.2.1. Description of Use

This section describes in detail the functionalities of *ProtoColl*. The novelty of this artifact is the combination of the features which are based on the design implications that have been described in Section 3.2 and Section 3.3. These features are:

- The implementation as a web-based lightweight application, which runs on any modern web browser.

- Collaboration with other users asynchronously and synchronously.

- The possibility to link the prototypes with other artifacts, other prototypes, and users.

- The application supports at the same time freehand sketches of prototypes and template GUI widgets.

4.2.1.1. Projects

To use *ProtoColl*, a user has to open its URL in a web browser. Then, the *ProtoColl* application loads and a login window appears. After logging in, *ProtoColl* shows the projects dialog. This can be seen in Figure 4.3.

ProtoColl supports multiple projects, as organizations often run multiple development projects in parallel. These projects can be created in this dialog. When creating a new project, a new name for the project has to be chosen and it appears in the project list. The user can open or delete projects in this list.

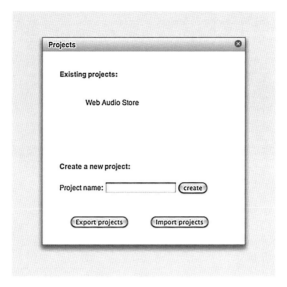

Figure 4.3.: The Projects Dialog

When the mouse pointer is moved over the project names, buttons for these actions appear at the side. Moreover, projects can be imported and exported with the respective buttons in the dialog.

When remote users create or delete projects the project list reflects these actions instantaneously. After clicking on the *open* button for a project, the dialog disappears and the content of the project is shown. A user can only open one project at a time, but different users can have different projects open at the same time. Furthermore, a project can be opened by multiple users at the same time for synchronous collaboration.

4.2.1.2. Creating Graphical Elements

Figure 4.4 depicts an overview of the *ProtoColl* application with a project opened. The screen is divided into several parts. In the center, there are

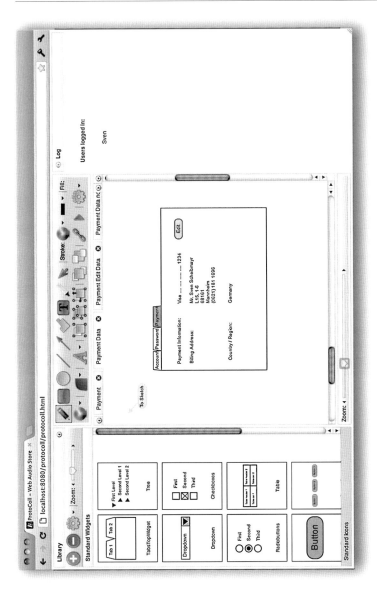

Figure 4.4.: Overview of the *ProtoColl* Application

multiple tabs with space for the prototypes. Each tab contains a surface, where graphical elements and UI widgets can be shown. These surfaces are called *canvases*. An arbitrary number of canvases can be created. When a canvas is created, a name has to be chosen, which is shown in its tab. On the canvases the prototypes are created from several graphical elements. Below the canvases, a zoom slider is located. The slider is used to resize everything on the canvas and the canvas itself. Every user can set her own zoom factor for the canvases.

In the following the use case of a payment functionality for a web shop exemplifies this. Figure 4.5 shows a freehand draft of the prototype for the payment functionality. The screen at the upper right side is used for editing credit card data and the billing address. This prototype is created with the pencil tool, which is the first tool in the toolbar of *ProtoColl*. The pencil tool simulates drawing with a physical pencil. This can be used to quickly save ideas and simulate the work with paper or a whiteboard. An intuitive way the pencil tool can be applied, is using a mobile device with a touchscreen or a graphics tablet.

ProtoColl also provides rectangle, ellipse, line, arrow, polygon, and text box tools. These tools can be used if a prototype is to be further refined, as can be seen with the prototype for the payment screen in Figure 4.6. In order to create graphical elements with these tools, the user selects the tool and then clicks and drags on the canvas. The rectangle and ellipse tools can also be used to create squares and circles. When the user drags on the canvas with the rectangle or ellipse tool selected and holds the shift key on the keyboard, a square or circle is created. The shift key can also be used when the line tool is selected for drawing lines horizontally, vertically or in a 45 degree angle.

The polygon tool can be used to create either polylines or polygons. A use case for this tool are the tab headers in Figure 4.6. The user selects the tool and clicks on the canvas to create a new point for the polygon or polyline. To finish the creation of the polygon or polyline the user double clicks to add the

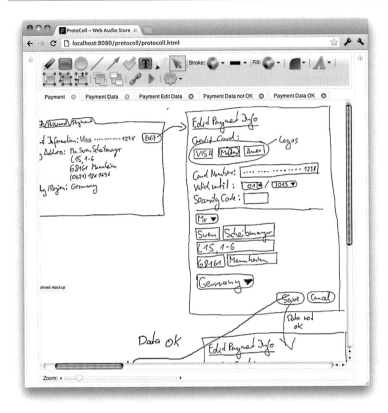

Figure 4.5.: Prototype Drawn with the Pencil Tool

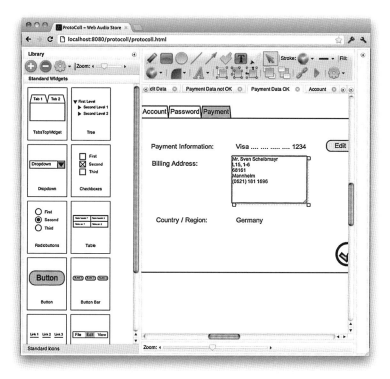

Figure 4.6.: Editing Text of a Text Box

last point. When this happens close to the first point, the polyline is closed and a polygon with a *fill* color is created.

A very common use case is the creation of text. It is created with the text box tool. A text box is created like a rectangle. The difference is that a text input field appears where the text can be entered, which is displayed within the bounds of the text box. Text boxes can contain single or multiple lines of text. When the text is too long to fit into the bounds of the rectangle it is wrapped automatically. To edit the text of an existing text box, the selection tool is used. The user can double click the box with the selection tool selected and the input field appears. This can be seen in Figure 4.6.

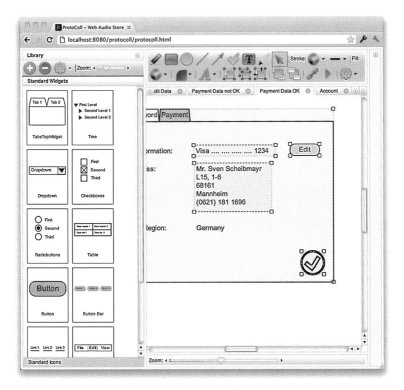

Figure 4.7.: Multiple Selections

The line color and width as well as the fill color of selected elements can be changed with drop down menus in the tool bar. The users can also change font sizes and the corner radius of text boxes and rectangles. A use case would be the creation of buttons, which often exhibit rounded corners.

To change the position or size of the shapes, like ellipses, rectangles or lines, the selection tool is used. The user clicks on a shape and small handles appear around the shape. These handles can be dragged and the shape is resized. This can be seen in Figure 4.7. Furthermore, multiple elements can be selected to change attributes (e.g., color or font sizes) at once or move the elements in one step. This works by clicking the elements and holding down the shift key. An example for multiple selections is shown in Figure 4.7.

4.2.1.3. GUI Widgets

GUI Widgets are GUI elements which represent a common functionality like dialog boxes, scroll bars, or menus. With *ProtoColl* users can create their own specific GUI widgets from simple graphical elements and store those into the library. Furthermore, they can use predefined template widgets, which can be adjusted for specific needs.

The creation of widgets is exemplified with the use case of a scrollbar. It is shown in a half-finished state in Figure 4.8. The scrollbar is made of several simple graphical elements like a rectangle and polylines. They are combined with the grouping feature of *ProtoColl*. To group several elements, the user has to select them and click on the group icon. When elements are grouped, they are treated like a single element and can be moved together. There can also exist groups of groups. To ungroup elements, the user selects the group and clicks the ungroup icon.

When creating GUI widgets from simple graphical elements, it must be defined how these elements react when the widget is resized. For this purpose *ProtoColl* provides a button in the toolbar to adjust the alignment of elements within a group. When a group is resized, the elements can be resized proportionally. Another possibility is to resize only some elements (e.g., a surrounding box) and position other elements (e.g., an icon within the box) in a fixed distance to the bounds of the group.

The scrollbar in Figure 4.8 comprises a simple box, which forms the outer bounds of the scrollbar and two icons with arrows at both ends of the bar. In the screenshot, only one icon has been created yet. When the length of the

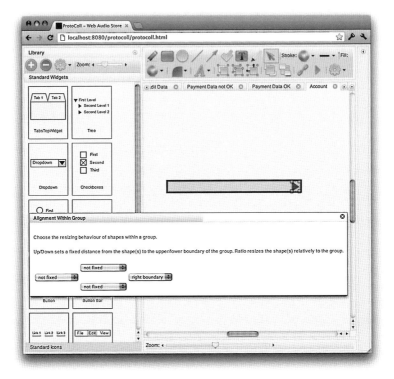

Figure 4.8.: Alignment Within a Group of Elements Dialog

scroll bar is adjusted, only the box should resize. The icons should stay at the end of the bar and its size should not change. This can be accomplished with the alignment dialog shown in the figure.

There are four drop down menus, which affect the four sides of the element. The options in the menu for the left and right side are: not fixed, ratio, left boundary, and right boundary. The options for the upper and lower side are: not fixed, ratio, upper boundary, and lower boundary. When not fixed is chosen, the element is neither repositioned nor resized when the group is resized. When ratio is chosen, the element is resized proportionally to the group. Left boundary, right boundary, upper boundary, and lower

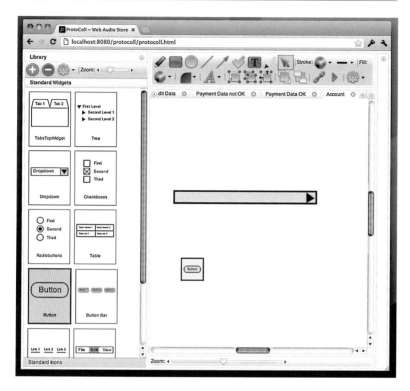

Figure 4.9.: The Library with the Standard Widgets Category Open

boundary means that the element is always positioned with a fixed distance to the respective boundary of the group.

In the scrollbar example of Figure 4.8, the attribute for the right side of the icon is changed to `right boundary`. Thus, the icon is always positioned with a fixed distance to the box of the scrollbar, which determines the boundaries of the bar. Therefore, the icon always stays at the end of the bar when the bar is resized and does not change its size, which is the desired behavior.

When new GUI widgets are created, they can be stored in the library. The library is located at the left sidebar of *ProtoColl*, which is shown in Figure 4.9. It can also be hidden. The widgets in the library can be reused in the same or

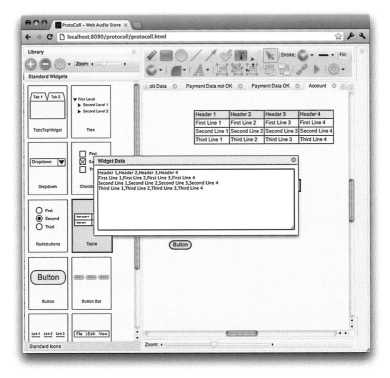

Figure 4.10.: Configuring a Table Widget

other projects. It is a common use case that elements should be reused, which makes the creation of prototypes more efficient. Users can organize items in the library into categories. The library can contain an arbitrary number of categories, which can be added or deleted by the users. They can also import or export the whole library.

The library contains predefined categories with GUI widgets or icons, which are provided by default. Figure 4.9 shows the category for the standard GUI widgets. There exist various standard widgets, like buttons, menus, tables, etc. Figure 4.9 also shows how a button is dragged out of the widget category onto the canvas. Drag and drop is the general way for adding items from the library to canvases.

When widgets from the standard widgets category are dragged onto a canvas, a dialog with a text input box appears where the widget can be configured. As an example, the dialog is shown for a table widget in Figure 4.10. The content of a widget is defined using a textual description. Figure 4.10 shows that each row of the table is defined by a row in the text input field. The columns of the table are separated with commas. When the dialog box is closed, the widget is updated.

4.2.1.4. Linking

Another important feature of *ProtoColl* is the ability to create links between elements on canvases and between these elements and artifacts outside the application. This is useful to provide context information for the prototypes. A use case could be a data entry mask prototype which is linked to a wiki page. The page documents the data format and how it is stored in the database. This feature is provided by two icons in the toolbar. The first icon, which resembles a chain, opens the link dialog for a selected element. This dialog is shown in Figure 4.11.

The link dialog has three different functionalities. First, it provides a URL for the selected element. This URL can be used within an external artifact to link back to the element. For example, the link could be used on a wiki page, which contains a textual requirements specification. When the user clicks on this link, the *ProtoColl* application loads and shows the element. The second feature is a list of links to external artifacts. An arbitrary number of links can be created. The user can enter a URL and a description for the link. This provides the opportunity to reference other artifacts from within a prototype.

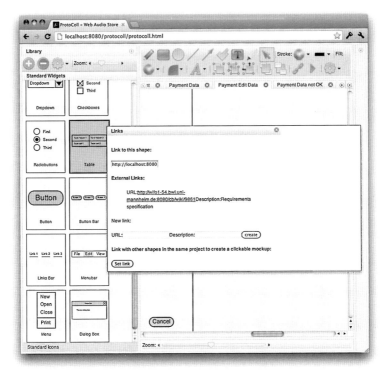

Figure 4.11.: Link Dialog

For instance, the user can look up further specifications for a GUI element with these links. These functionalities to create bidirectional links are important to support contextualization (see Section 3.1.2).

The last feature of the link dialog is the possibility to create links from an element on the canvas to another element, which could possibly be on another canvas. This enables the user to create prototypes which can simulate a sequence of screens and thus dynamic behavior setting prototypes in context of other prototypes. When the user clicks the *set link* button, the link dialog disappears and *ProtoColl* enters a special mode. Below the toolbar, a section

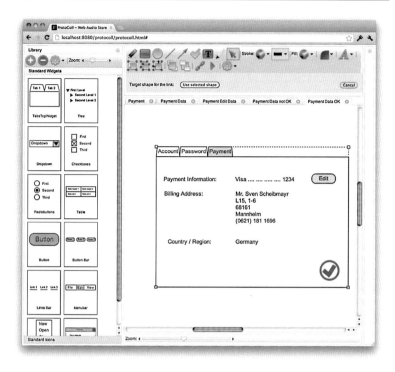

Figure 4.12.: Internal Linking Mode

appears, containing buttons to use a selected element as the link target or to
cancel and exit the mode. This can be seen in Figure 4.12.

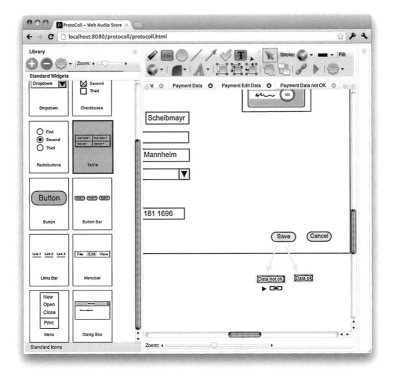

Figure 4.13.: Link Icon of an Element

When an element on a canvas has a link to another element, a triangle icon
resembling an arrow head, is displayed as soon as the user moves the mouse
pointer over this element. This is shown in Figure 4.13. When the user clicks
on this icon, *ProtoColl* shows the target element. Furthermore, next to the
triangle icon, an icon resembling a chain is displayed. This icon can also be
used to open the link dialog.

4.2.1.5. Collaboration

ProtoColl allows multiple users to work together synchronously on one project. All actions on the canvas or in the library are instantaneously synchronized between the users. This ensures that all users always work with the same current state of the prototypes. A use case could be a project manager and a developer creating a prototype while talking via a video conference. The project manager contributes client requirements, while the developer provides more technical knowledge about the feasibility of the features and the GUI. Both can create and change GUI elements and widgets at the same time.

To provide awareness to the users of the actions of other users *ProtColl* shows user names next to graphical elements. When a user selects shapes on the canvas, these selections are indicated at the remote users' sites with the name of the selecting user next to the selected shapes (see Figure 4.14).

Furthermore, users can use a special tool that is called the marker tool to provide awareness. The marker tool shows a temporary highlight on the canvas. It simulates a text marker and can be used to direct other users' attention to an element. After a few seconds, the highlight fades away. An example for a highlight can be seen in Figure 4.15. This screenshot also shows the synchronization with other users, which is in this case simulated by opening two browser windows.

For presenting purposes, the simulation of a sequence of screens can be shared with remote users. When working synchronously with other users in *ProtoColl*, a user can click on the play icon in the toolbar, which is located next to the icon for the link dialog. This icon resembles an arrow head. When the icon is clicked, *ProtoColl* enters the play mode. In this mode, remote users can follow the sequence of screens, which appear when the user clicks on links, as the remote users' views are synchronized.

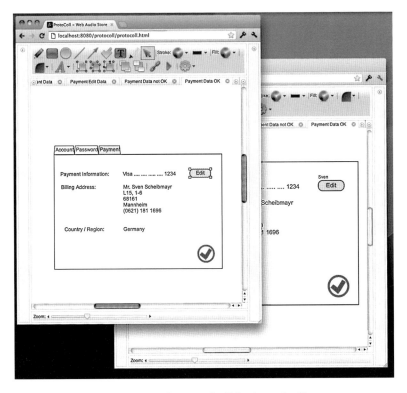

Figure 4.14.: Indicating the Selections of a User

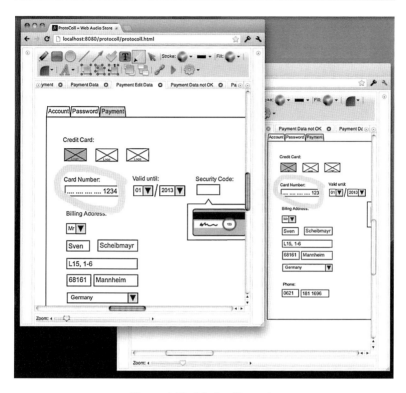

Figure 4.15.: Marker Example

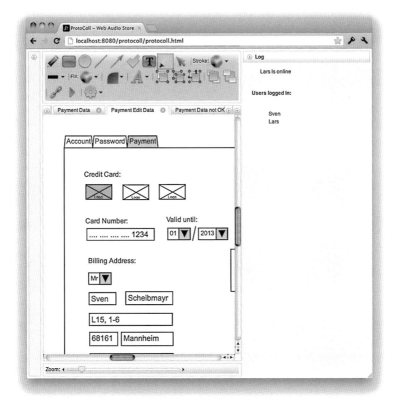

Figure 4.16.: Log Sidebar

At the right side of the *ProtoColl* window, the log sidebar is located. It is hidden by the icon in the upper left of the bar to save screen space. The log shows all users who have the project currently open (see Figure 4.16). Furthermore, it shows when users come online or go offline.

When users collaborate asynchronously, a history of all user activities can be shown in the log. This can be used to look at earlier versions of the prototypes and see which changes have been made by individual users. A use case could be a team of requirement engineers and developers creating a prototype together. The next day the project manager reviews the prototype and requires more information for a specific feature. She can look into the log and see who created the relevant part of the prototype and contact this person.

4.2.2. Technologies

4.2.2.1. Web Platform

As noted in Section 3.3, one design implication for the tool is that it must be lightweight. This design implication is realized with a web-based solution. As the tool runs in any modern web browser[6], it does not have to be installed on the client systems. This gives stakeholders easy access to the tool and avoids complicated installation procedures. Moreover, it enables stakeholders who do not have the possibility to install software on their client machines to access the service. This advantage is especially important for stakeholders of the client organization or users of the to be developed software system who have to work with the IT infrastructure of their own organization.

Furthermore, the tool can be accessed on various platforms, like Windows, Linux, or Macintosh systems, without modifications. Also mobile devices, like tablets, can be used. Moreover, as the browser always loads the newest version of the tool, update management is effortless for the user. Because of these advantages of a lightweight browser-based solution, it becomes possible to give a wider range of stakeholders access to the software tool, than with a heavyweight desktop application.

As a web-based application *ProtoColl* uses fundamental technologies of the web, such as the Hypertext Markup Language (HTML) and JavaScript. HTML

---

6 Browsers which are supported must be able to run the JavaScript framework Dojo (see http://dojotoolkit.org/, accessed 07/02/2012) in version 1.6.1 or higher and support an Application Programming Interface (API) used by Dojo to draw vector graphics (Scalable Vector Graphics (SVG), Canvas, Silverlight, etc.) (see http://dojotoolkit.org/reference-guide/1.8/dojox/gfx.html, accessed 09/23/2012).

is used to render the user interface elements of the tool. This means, everything the user sees and interacts with, except the actual mockups, is rendered
with HTML. The mockups are drawn with a vector graphics Application Programming Interface (API), supported by modern web browsers. On the client
side, i.e., in the web browser (see Section 4.2.3), the application is written in
JavaScript, which is the main part of the application. It consists of over 15.000
lines of JavaScript code. In the recent years, the performance of JavaScript
engines built into the web browsers has improved significantly due to fierce
competition between the web browser vendors (Ratanaworabhan et al., 2010).
This enabled the development of web applications, whose performance is on par
with desktop applications.

The interface of JavaScript in the browser is the Document Object Model
(DOM). It represents the elements of the HTML document as JavaScript objects, which can be manipulated. With this mechanism, JavaScript can be used
to dynamically change the document in the browser, which represents the user
interface of the web application, as user-invoked events occur. The DOM API
provides only low level methods to access and manipulate the content of the
HTML document. Furthermore, there still exist several incompatibilities between browsers by different vendors, which have to be addressed. Due to this,
various JavaScript libraries have been developed. These libraries implement
functionalities to work around browser incompatibilities and provide higher
level functions, such as user interface widgets.

4.2.2.2. Dojo

ProtoColl is built upon the widely used JavaScript library Dojo[7], which is applied in various ways. It is used to manipulate the DOM and to change the

---

7 http://dojotoolkit.org/ (accessed 07/02/2012)

styles of HTML elements dynamically, which changes the appearance of the user interface. Furthermore, Dojo provides a way to consistently subscribe to mouse events, which still is an area of incompatibilities between browser vendors. *ProtoColl* also uses a publish-subscribe-mechanism of Dojo to simplify routing of messages between JavaScript objects. As JavaScript uses the concept of prototypes for object orientation, where objects are cloned to provide reuse of functionality, Dojo implements its own mechanism to apply class-based object orientation. *ProtoColl* uses this mechanism throughout the whole application. Moreover, Dojo provides a system to modularize the application into components, which is also used.

Another part of Dojo, which is often used in *ProtoColl*, are the user interface widgets, called *Dijits*[8]. These are used to draw toolbars, buttons, sliders, tabs, dialog boxes and to divide the layout of *ProtoColl*'s user interface into several parts. Dojo uses multiple HTML elements and Cascading Style Sheets (CSS) to render these user interface widgets. This widget system simplifies the creation of the web application's user interface via JavaScript, and further provides the possibility to effortless change the interface's appearance with various themes and adapt its text elements to the users' local language.

4.2.2.3. Vector Graphics

One of the most important parts of *ProtoColl* is the display and editing of the user interface prototypes. *ProtoColl* needs to render these mockups in the browser. The mockups consist of various types of shapes, like e.g., lines, polygons, ellipses and rectangles. These shapes can be very complex, as for example when resembling pen strokes. Furthermore, *ProtoColl* supports a zoom functionality, which enables the user to view details of the mockup or get an overview

---

8 http://dojotoolkit.org/reference-guide/1.7/dijit/index.html
  (accessed 07/02/2012)

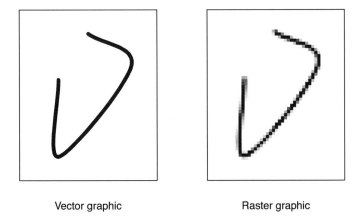

Vector graphic   Raster graphic

Figure 4.17.: Vector Graphic Versus Raster Graphic

by zooming out. To fulfill these graphical requirements, vector graphics technology is used, which is supported by modern web browsers. Vector graphics consist of graphical primitives, such as lines, curves, polygons, which are represented by mathematical expressions. This can be contrasted with raster images, which store the color of individual pixels to represent the image. Vector graphics can be magnified without any loss of quality, whereas raster images lose detail and become blurry when they are magnified. This is illustrated in Figure 4.17.

Dojo provides a vector graphics library called Dojox.gfx[9], which can use – depending on the browser support – different underlying web technologies to render the graphics. One technology Dojox.gfx can use are Scalable Vector Graphics (SVG)[10], which is a standard developed and maintained by the Word Wide Web Consortium (W3C)[11]. It is a format based on the Extensible Markup Language (XML) to represent vector graphics. SVG is supported by the current

---

9 http://dojotoolkit.org/reference-guide/1.7/dojox/gfx.html (accessed 07/02/2012)
10 http://www.w3.org/Graphics/SVG/ (accessed 07/02/2012)
11 http://www.w3.org/ (accessed 07/02/2012)

versions of the web browsers Internet Explorer[12], Firefox[13], Safari[14], Opera[15], and Chrome[16]. Furthermore it is supported by the current mobile versions of Safari[17] and Opera[18] and by the Android Browser[19]. If SVG is not supported by the browser, other technologies can be used. In older versions of Internet Explorer (version 8.0 and below), Vector Markup Language (VML) can be used, which is also an XML-based format. Another feasible rendering engine is Microsoft's proprietary technology Silverlight[20] as well as HTML5's canvas element[21]. Although different rendering engines can be used to draw the graphics, this is transparent to the application using Dojox.gfx, i.e., *ProtoColl*, as the code does not have to be modified. This enables *ProtoColl* to run on many different browsers on a variety of desktop and mobile platforms, without any additional effort to change the application's code.

4.2.2.4. Comet

In order to support synchronous work, *ProtoColl* must be able to send and receive updates about the state of the application to other users. This is realized with the fundamental mechanics and protocols of the web, such as the Hypertext Transfer Protocol (HTTP). The HTTP protocol works with a request and response mechanism. The web browser sends a request to the server and the server answers with a response message. There are different types of requests, such as requests to retrieve a resource (e.g. a HTML file) from the server (a

---

12 http://windows.microsoft.com/en-us/internet-explorer/products/ie/home (accessed 07/03/2012)
13 http://www.mozilla.org/en-US/firefox/new/ (accessed 07/03/2012)
14 http://www.apple.com/safari/ (accessed 07/03/2012)
15 http://www.opera.com/ (accessed 07/03/2012)
16 https://www.google.com/intl/en/chrome/browser/ (accessed 07/03/2012)
17 http://www.apple.com/iphone/built-in-apps/safari.html (accessed 07/03/2012)
18 http://www.opera.com/mobile/ (accessed 07/03/2012)
19 http://www.android.com/about/ (accessed 07/03/2012)
20 http://www.silverlight.net/ (accessed 07/03/2012)
21 http://www.w3.org/TR/2dcontext/ (accessed 07/03/2012)

GET request) or requests to create a new resource (e.g. submitting a form with data on a web page) on the server (a POST request).

On web pages, the user clicks on a hyperlink and the web browser sends a GET request to the web server. The server sends the requested resources as a response and the web browser reloads the whole page and displays these resources (e.g., html document, images, etc.). Due to this reload of the whole page, this mechanism is inefficient for web applications where often only small parts have to be updated during usage. Because of this, modern web applications use a set of technologies, called Asynchronous JavaScript and XML (Ajax), to retrieve data from the server and update the user interface without a page reload (Paulson, 2005).

Ajax-based applications use the XMLHttpRequest JavaScript object[22] to make a request to the web server and retrieve data without a page reload (Ajax calls). The XMLHttpRequest object is supported in all modern web browsers. Despite of the name of the XMLHttpRequest object, it is not restricted to XML data. In fact, it can be used to transfer data of any format. A common format used by web applications is JavaScript Object Notation (JSON)[23]. JSON is a text based format for structured data. It is based on the Syntax of JavaScript and thus, can be easily parsed by the JavaScript interpreter in the browser. *ProtoColl* uses the JSON format for message exchange between the clients and the server.

Ajax improves the efficiency of a single user web applications, but multi-user web applications need extended functionality to enable efficient collaboration. Users of a collaborative web application employ web browsers (the clients) to connect to the a web server (the server) (see Figure 4.20 in Section 4.2.3). When a user changes the state of the application, this change has to be propagated

---

22 http://www.w3.org/TR/XMLHttpRequest/ (accessed 07/05/2012)
23 http://www.json.org/ (accessed 07/05/2012)

through the server to all other clients. Thus, the server has to be able to push updates to the clients. This reaction on server side events is not possible with the traditional request-response-model of common web pages or Ajax-based web applications. To make server side event pushing possible, techniques have been developed which use a long living HTTP connection. Several names, like Ajax Push or Reverse Ajax, have been used for these techniques (Crane and McCarthy, 2008). The most prominent name is Comet, which has been coined by Google developer Alex Russell in 2006[24].

The idea is to open an HTTP connection to the server and keep the connection open. When an event on the server occurs, it is transmitted via this connection. Depending on the implementation, the connection remains open after the event or the client closes and reopens it and waits for further events. The implementation details depend on browser support and can be realized with e.g., hidden iframes or XMLHttpRequests. Another possibility is the new W3C standard WebSocket, which provides a dedicated bidirectional connection via the Transmission Control Protocol (TCP).

ProtoColl builds on the comet solution CometD[25] by the Dojo Foundation[26]. CometD provides a Java web server, based on the Jetty project[27], which implements comet functionality. Furthermore, it provides a JavaScript library, which facilitates the use of comet on the client. CometD abstracts from browser particularities and uses the best technology that is available in the browser like WebSocket, XMLHttpRequests, etc. Furthermore, it implements the Bayeux protocol[28], which defines a message routing mechanism to distribute messages

---

24 http://infrequently.org/2006/03/comet-low-latency-data-for-the-browser/ (accessed 07/08/2012)
25 http://cometd.org/ (accessed 07/08/2012)
26 http://dojofoundation.org/ (accessed 07/08/2012)
27 http://eclipse.org/jetty/ (accessed 07/08/2012)
28 http://cometd.org/documentation/bayeux/spec (accessed 07/09/2012)

from the clients to the server, from the server to the clients, or from the clients
to other clients via the server.

The messages are transported with the comet technology via named channels. It uses a publish-subscribe mechanism, which allows clients to publish
messages to a channel and subscribe to channels. When a client subscribes to
a channel, all messages which are published to this channels are delivered to
this client. The publisher does not have to know which clients subscribed to
the channel and the subscribers do not have to know the publishers. With this
message distribution mechanism and the ability to use transportation technologies transparently to push the messages from the server to the clients, CometD
facilitates the development of collaborative web applications.

4.2.2.5. Operational Transformations

ProtoColl, as a web application, needs to be able to work with network connec-
tions whose latency is not always predictable and can be significant at times.
Hence, the actions the user performs should be performed immediately on the
client. The local state of *ProtoColl* is changed instantly and then the change
is propagated to other users via the network. This mechanism can lead to
consistency problems. In order to solve such problems, the operational transformation technology has been developed (Ellis and Gibbs, 1989; Ressel et al.,
1996; Sun et al., 1998; Xia et al., 2004). When two or more users change the
state of the application at the same time, this can lead to inconsistent states.
This is illustrated in Figure 4.18, where user Bob and user Alice change both
the text string acd.

Alice changes it to abcd, inserting a b at position 1 (OP1). Bob changes it
to cd, deleting the character a at position 0 (OP2). The changes are executed
locally instantly, but the propagation of the changes needs some time, which

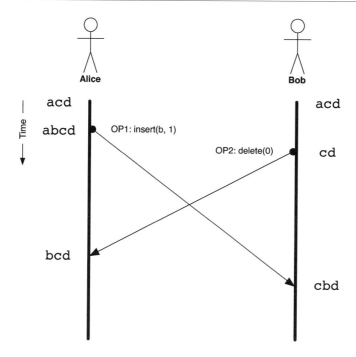

Figure 4.18.: Changes Leading to an Inconsistency

leads to an inconsistency. The insert operation of Alice inserts the b after the c on Bob's side, because the string was changed by Bob in the meantime. This results in the string bcd on Alice's side and the string cbd on Bob's side. In order to correct the inconsistency of Figure 4.18, OP1 of Alice has to be transformed. This is shown in Figure 4.19.

Instead of inserting the b at position 1, it is inserted at position 0. This corrects the inconsistency and the result is the string bcd on both sides. The idea of operational transformations is to transform the parameters of the operations depending on earlier operations which were executed. In this example, the position parameter of OP1 is transformed from 1 to 0 according to the earlier operation OP2.

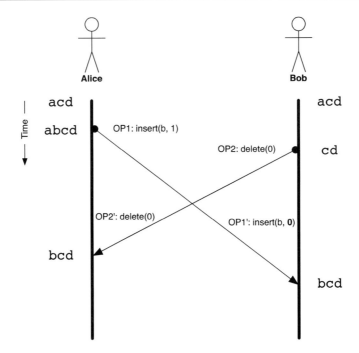

Figure 4.19.: Transformation of Operation 1 to Fix the Inconsistency

Operational transformations have been researched for several years (see, e.g., Ellis and Gibbs, 1989; Ressel et al., 1996; Sun et al., 1998; Xia et al., 2004). They have also be used in several implementations, e.g., the collaborative text editors SubEthaEdit[29] and Google Docs[30]. As operational transformations have been shown to be robust, *ProtoColl* uses this technology to synchronize its application state. The framework Open Cooperative Web Framework (OpenCoweb)[31], which is supported by the Dojo Foundation and implements a operational transformation engine, is used. It is divided in two parts: a Java-based collaboration server, which builds upon ComedD and a JavaScript library. The JavaScript

---

29 `http://www.codingmonkeys.de/subethaedit/index.html` (accessed 07/10/2012)
30 `http://docs.google.com` (accessed 07/10/2012)
31 `http://opencoweb.org/` (accessed 07/10/2012)

library is used to send and receive events for synchronization. The collaboration server receives JSON formatted event messages sent from the JavaScript library on the clients and pushes them to all other clients.

4.2.2.6. Persistence

In Section 3.2, it was outlined that the users of *ProtoColl* should be able to work synchronously and asynchronously. In order to support asynchronous collaboration, the application's state must be stored persistently on the server. The server part of the OpenCoweb framework used by *ProtoColl* only handles the passing and transformation of the cooperative event messages. It does not model the application state and has no functionality for persistence. Thus, another mechanism must be implemented to enable persistency.

ProtoColl opts for a virtual client solution, as can be seen in Figure 4.20 in Section 4.2.3.1. The JavaScript code of the *ProtoColl* client application is executed in a server side environment. This enables maximum code reuse, as all the *model* and *controller* classes can be reused (see Section 4.2.3.2). The *view* classes are not reused, because the server does not display any information. The `collaborationController` class was modified to implement persistency.

ProtoColl uses the JavaScript interpreter environment PhantomJS[32] for the server side execution of the JavaScript code. PhantomJS is based on WebKit[33], the web browser engine used by e.g., the web browsers Safari and Chrome. It can load the HTML, CSS and JavaScript code of a common web page or web application, execute it and render its results. It effectively emulates a web browser on the server. Even as there exist other environments for the execution of JavaScript code on the server (e.g., Node.js[34]), PhantomJS is a

---

32 `http://phantomjs.org/` (accessed 07/23/2012)
33 `http://www.webkit.org/` (accessed 07.23.2012)
34 `http://nodejs.org/` (accessed 07.23.2012)

simple solution to run code which was intended to be executed by a web browser on the server. This has the advantage, that the OpenCoweb JavaScript library can be used without any modification.

There are two implementations of PhantomJS, a C++ and a Python implementation. *ProtoColl* uses the Python implementation (PyPhantomJS[35]), which supports an interface between the JavaScript code and plugins that are written in Python. The plugins implement functions which write and read collaboration messages and application state information to a database in order to support persistence. These functions are called from the JavaScript code when collaboration messages are received or the application state has to be stored or recovered. They connect to a MySQL[36] database, which is a popular open source database technology. Moreover, the plugins are used when the history of the application state changes has to be looked up in the database. This enables the traceability of the users' actions. It can be shown how the mockups evolved and which person in the project changed them (see Section 4.1).

4.2.2.7. Summary of Technologies

In summary *ProtoColl* uses several state-of-the-art technologies to implement contemporary functionalities as a web application. Among these technologies are web technologies, like HTML and the DOM, which are used for the GUI of *ProtoColl*. Moreover, JavaScript is used as a programming language for the *ProtoColl* client application. Among other things, the JavaScript framework Dojo has been used to create the widgets for the GUI of *ProtoColl*. Comet and operational transformations have been used to implement *ProtoColl*'s synchronous collaboration functionality. This has been supported by the OpenCoweb frame-

---

35 https://github.com/kanzure/pyphantomjs (accessed 07/25/2012)
36 http://www.mysql.com/ (accessed 07/29/2012)

Table 4.1.: Technologies Used by *ProtoColl*

Technology	Function
HTML	Application GUI
JavaScript	Programming language for the client
DOM	Application GUI
Dojo	General purpose Javascript framework, application GUI widgets, vector graphics drawing
Comet	Pushing messages from the server to the client
Operational transformations	Ensuring application state consistency
OpenCoweb	Synchronous collaboration
PhantomJS	Virtual client environment, asynchronous collaboration, persistence
Python	Interface between JavaScript and data base
MySQL	Persistence

work. For the persistence and asynchronous collaboration features PhantomJS, Python, and MySQL have been used. Table 4.1 summarizes these technologies.

4.2.3. Architecture

4.2.3.1. Architecture Overview

The overall architecture of the *ProtoColl* system is a client-server-architecture (Berson, 1996), which is depicted in Figure 4.20. The clients can be desktop clients, which run operating systems such as Microsoft Windows, Apple OS X, or a Linux distribution. The only requirement is a contemporary web browser like Chrome, Safari, or Firefox.

Furthermore, clients can also be mobile devices, such as tablets, which also run web browsers. The advantage of a tablet device is the possibility to enter data with a pen directly on the screen. When creating freehand sketches of mockups, this is a more natural input method than the input with a mouse or trackpad. It simulates the quick and effortless creation of paper prototypes,

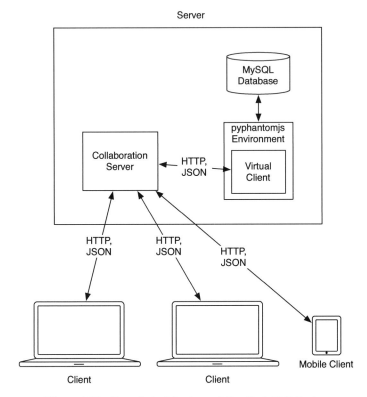

Figure 4.20.: Overall Architecture of the *ProtoColl* System

which are often used in practice, at least at the beginning of a project. The clients communicate with the server via the network. For this communication, web protocols are used, which transmit the collaborative messages.

As described in Section 4.2.2.6, *ProtoColl* uses a virtual virtual client architecture. An adapted instance of the *ProtoColl* application, which does not implement any graphical output, runs on the server in a PyPhantomJS environment (see Figure 4.20). This environment simulates a web browser on the server. Like the other clients, it communicates with the collaboration server via HTTP and JSON messages. It reacts to the actions of the other clients and replicates their application states. Moreover, it connects to a MySQL database to store these actions persistently.

ProtoColl is based on the Model-View-Controller (MVC) architectural pattern (Krasner and Pope, 1988). The MVC pattern enables a more flexible design of the application. It facilitates extension and reuse of its components. The *model* in MVC is the component which contains the data that the application processes and stores. There can be one or more objects which model this data. These objects implement methods to add, delete, and change the data. The *model* is independent of the *view* and the *controller* components, and does not have to have any knowledge about them. It does not implement any user interface. It is the *view's* function to present the data in the *model* to the user. It can present all or only parts of the data. Furthermore, multiple different *views* presenting the data in various ways can exist. The *controller* receives user inputs and processes them. It reacts to mouse clicks and keyboard events and also manages a *view*. In reaction to user inputs the *controller* can change the data in the *model* and manipulate the *view*.

4.2.3.2. Architecture Details

4.2.3.2.1. Projects Figure 4.21 shows a simplified diagram of the classes in *ProtoColl*. It only shows the most important classes with their class names and their relationships. In the upper part of the diagram the *model*, *view* and *controller* classes can be seen. For instance, it is shown that the `Projects Controller` class has a relationship to the `ProjectsDialog` class (its *view*) and the `ProjectsModel` class. It instantiates its *model* and its *view* and passes a reference of the *model* to the *view*. The *view* uses this reference to get the names of the projects from the *model* to display them in a list. The dialog which the *view* shows is displayed in Figure 4.3. The `ProjectsController` also passes a reference of itself to the *view*, which the *view* uses to communicate those actions that the user executes (adding and removing projects) to the *controller*. The *controller* acts as a mediator between the *view* and the *model* and invokes the public methods of the *model* for adding and removing projects.

When the `ProjectsController` adds or removes projects, it also instantiates or destroys new `ProjectController` objects and keeps references to these objects. Thus, a composition relationship between the `ProjectsController` class and the `ProjectController` class is displayed in Figure 4.21. Furthermore, `ProjectController` publishes the adding and removing of the projects via the Dojo publish/subscribe mechanism. This notifications are used by the `CollaborationController` to inform remote clients about the changes and synchronize their states. The publication is not active when *ProtoColl* is running as a virtual client on the server (see Figure 4.20 in Section 4.2.3) because the virtual client only synchronizes its state in response to user actions on client devices. It does not create, update, or delete projects on its own. Thus, the *controller* class is changed for the virtual client version of *ProtoColl* and the publication is disabled.

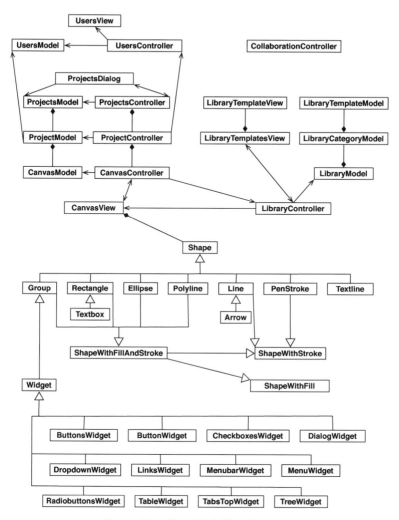

Figure 4.21.: Simplified Class Diagram

The other *model*, *view*, and *controller* classes as shown in Figure 4.21 provide similar functionalities as `ProjectsModel`, `ProjectsDialog`, and `Projects Controller` do for the objects they manage and display. As said, there is a composition relationship between the `ProjectsController` class and the `ProjectController` class. Corresponding to that, there is a composition relationship between the `ProjectsModel` and the `ProjectModel` class, as the overall projects *model* contains the *models* of the individual projects. One level deeper, each project can contain multiple canvases on which *ProtoColl* draws the graphical elements. Thus, there are also composition relationships between the `ProjectModel` and `CanvasModel` classes as well as between the `ProjectController` and `CanvasController` classes.

The `ProjectController` class contains methods for managing the opening state of a project. When a project is opened, the `ProjectController` subscribes to the actions of the toolbar and tells its `CanvasController` objects to show the canvases' *views*. The `ProjectController` also stores a reference of MVC classes for user management. These classes manage the users which have opened the project. The user names of these users are shown in a pane in the log side bar. Furthermore, `ProjectController` implements methods to add and remove canvases locally or to react on adding and removing actions of remote users. It instantiates or destroys the respective `CanvasModel`, `CanvasView`, and `CanvasController` objects and publishes these actions to remote users similar to the `ProjectsController` class. Other functionality that the `ProjectController` class contains is copying canvases as well as providing the ability to link elements on different canvases and follow these links.

4.2.3.2.2. Drawing Surfaces   The `CanvasController` class provides similar functionalities as `ProjectsController` and `ProjectController` for the canvas level. It implements methods for creating and destroying its *view* and adding, removing, and updating shapes locally and via remote users. Furthermore, the `CanvasController` handles the selections of shapes. `CanvasController` publishes these selections to remote users and shows selections of remote users to the local user. Another functionality of `CanvasController` is handling the creation of markers by local and remote users.

A very important class is `CanvasView`. It implements all functionalities for managing the graphical shapes on the drawing surface. It creates a drawing surface with the help of Dojox.gfx (see Section 4.2.2). Often, this will be based on SVG, but other technologies are possible, if the client's browser supports them. `CanvasView` manages an array in which references of shape objects are stored. The order of the shape objects in this array corresponds to the order of the shapes. The class also reacts on mouse and keyboard events, which are executed by the user. Furthermore, it manages subscriptions to events of the toolbar and activates them if it is the active canvas. In addition, it subscribes to the events from the zoom slider. For zooming a method to resize the drawing surface and all its graphical shapes is implemented. Moreover, `CanvasView` provides methods for copying shapes, grouping and ungrouping multiple shapes, and moving shapes to the background and to the front. Furthermore, it implements a method which scrolls the *view* to a specific shape. This is used when the user clicks on a link, which points to this shape.

4.2.3.2.3. Shapes The shape objects in the array, which `CanvasView` manages, all inherit from the class **Shape** as illustrated in Figure 4.21. This class implements many methods which are universal for all shapes. Furthermore, it declares some methods which subclasses have to override. There are methods for handling mouse events and moving the shape on the canvas. In addition, it implements methods for updating and reading data which is available for all shapes. It also contains drawing functionality. A selection box can be drawn around shapes and link icons and user names can be drawn next to shapes. The subclasses of shapes implement further specific methods for drawing, e.g., rectangles, lines, or text and handling user actions on these graphical elements. For example, the Rectangle class implements methods for drawing handles at the corners of the rectangle. The user can drag these handles and, thus, resize the rectangle. The class Textbox inherits from Rectangle. It draws text within the bounds of a rectangle and implements methods for line wrapping.

Some shapes draw graphical elements only with an outline (*stroke*) color while other shapes draw their elements with an additional *fill* color. Therefore, there is the class ShapeWithStroke, which reacts to toolbar actions for changing the *stroke* color. The corresponding class for the *fill* color is ShapeWithFill. It exists a class ShapeWithFillAndStroke, which inherits from both of these classes and is used for shapes with both, a *stroke* and a *fill*. These are the classes Group, Rectangle, Textbox, Ellipse, and Polyline. Classes which directly or indirectly inherit only from ShapeWithStroke are Line, Arrow, and PenStroke. The class Textline neither inherits from ShapeWithStroke nor from ShapeWithFill, as it only draws a line of text.

The class Group implements functionality for managing multiple shapes combined as one group. It contains methods for calculating the overall bounds of all the grouped shapes and for drawing handles or a selection outline. Furthermore, it implements special functionality for resizing groups. The Widget class is a subclass of Group. This is the super class for all predefined user interface widgets, which are available in the library. It implements some universal methods for changing the font size and colors of the widget and for resizing it. Furthermore, it implements the functionality for editing the text of a widget that defines its content. This can be a single line of text for, e.g., a button or multiple text lines for, e.g., a menu.

Widget shows a text editing box, when the user double clicks on the widget. All subclasses of Widget implement a method createWidget which parses this text and creates and accordingly positions the shapes that together form the whole widget. The subclasses of widget, which are implemented in *Proto-Coll*, are: ButtonsWidget, ButtonWidget, CheckboxesWidget, DialogWidget, DropdownWidget, LinksWidget, MenubarWidget, MenuWidget, Radiobuttons Widget, TableWidget, TabsTopWidget, TreeWidget. It is easily possible to extend this collection of widgets by subclassing the Widget class and implementing the createWidget method.

4.2.3.2.4. Library

CanvasController references the LibraryController. This class is responsible for the management of the library. LibraryController implements methods for instantiating the *views* for the categories (Library TemplatesView), which then instantiate the *views* for the templates (Library TemplateView), and for adding and removing categories and templates. When categories and templates are added or removed, their *models* (LibraryCategory Model and LibraryTemplateModel) are added to or removed from Library Model. Furthermore, the adding and removing actions are published to remote users. LibraryController also notices when remote users add or remove categories or templates. Another functionality that LibraryController implements is inserting a template into a canvas by dragging it out of a category and dropping it onto a canvas.

4.2.3.2.5. Collaboration

ProtoColl uses the OpenCoweb framework as a collaboration engine (see Section 4.2.2). On the client-side, the collaboration Controller class publishes cooperative event messages to the server and subscribes to certain channels in order to receive the messages from the server and further process them. This is done via the objects provided by the OpenCoweb JavaScript library. The events have several attributes. These are name, value, type, and position. When a client subscribes for a specific event, it uses the name attribute as an identifier.

Furthermore, the collaboration engine uses the `name` attribute to determine other possibly conflicting events. Only events with the same name can be conflicting. When subscribing to an event, the name can contain the wildcard character `*`, allowing the subscription to multiple events. The handling of the creation of projects by remote clients is an example where this mechanism is used in *ProtoColl*. The client subscribes to the events with the name `protocoll.projects.*`. This results in a subscription to all events having names that start with `protocoll.projects.` and end with an arbitrary character sequence of zero or more characters. As the *ProtoColl* client appends the unique identifier of a project to the name, the subscription to `protocoll.projects.*` subscribes to all project creation events.

The `value` attribute is the actual data being transmitted. Hence, in *ProtoColl* this attribute can contain data which describes a graphical shape in the mockup. If the collaboration engine detects a conflict between multiple events – e.g., two users changing a shape at the same time – it resolves this conflict by changing (transforming) the `values` of the events. The `type` of the event determines which kind of operation is executed and how the event is transformed in the case of a conflict. There are four types of events: `insert`, `delete`, `update`, and `null` type.

The `insert` type is used when a new object is created, e.g. a user creates a new graphical shape in a mockup. The `delete` type is used when an object is removed and the `update` type is used when attributes of an object are changed, e.g., the color of a shape is changed from black to red. `Null` types are used when the event cannot be conflicting with another event. In the case of a `null` type event, the operational transformation engine is bypassed.

OpenCoweb supports a one-dimensional data structure for the collaboration (e.g., an array or a string). Hence, when creating, deleting, or changing objects, `position` as an additional attribute must be provided. *ProtoColl* uses this to

Table 4.2.: Example Insert Operation of a Shape on the Canvas at Position 3

attribute	attribute value
name	`protocoll.project.shape.2122781039215624313333`
value	`<shape data>`
type	`insert`
position	`3`

allow users to collaborate on a set of graphical shapes. The shapes are added to an array as they are created by the users. An example operation could be the insertion of a shape at position 3 as shown in Table 4.2.

The `position` attribute can be transformed by the operational transformation engine when conflicts occur. Figure 4.22 exemplifies this. Two users work on two different client machines and edit the graphical shapes of a mockup. User 1 updates shape 2 (s_2) and user 2 deletes shape 1 (s_1). As *ProtoColl* stores all shapes of a mockup in an array, the position of the shape which is to be updated or deleted must be specified. At the start, shape 1 is at position 0, shape 2 is at position 1, and shape 3 is at position 2. Hence, operation 1 (OP1) of user 1 is an operation of `type insert` with the attribute `position 1`. Operation 2 (OP2) of user 2 is an operation of `type delete` with the attribute `position 0`. As both operations are performed at about the same time and the transmission of the operations via the network takes time, the result would be an inconsistency, if no transformation was performed. To avoid that, the operational transformation engine transforms the attribute `position` of operation 1. This results in operation 1' (OP1') having the attribute `position` set to the value 0. Now the correct shape is updated on the side of user 2. Operation 2 is not modified by the transformation engine.

In order to avoid inconsistencies, the operational transformation engine transforms events according to earlier events, which have already been received. The change might affect the `value` or the `position` attribute. Furthermore, the

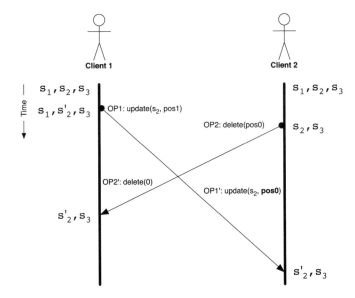

Figure 4.22.: Example of an Operational Transformation Performed When Shapes Are Edited in *ProtoColl*

Table 4.3.: Possible Transformations of Cooperative Events

	insert	delete	update
insert	position	position	no transformation
delete	position	position / drop	no transformation
update	position	position / drop	value

event can be dropped entirely. Table 4.3 shows all possible transformations[37]. Events in the rows are the current events, which are about to be transformed. Events in the columns are events which have been received earlier.

4.2.3.2.6. Creating Shapes When user actions are executed, multiple objects are affected in *ProtoColl*. Actions like adding, removing, or updating shapes can originate from the local user or from remote users. Figure 4.23 shows a sequence diagram for the creation of a generic shape by a local user. There are four *ProtoColl* objects which take part in the creation process. These are objects of the following classes: Shape, CanvasView, CanvasController, and CanvasModel. Furthermore, the Dojo and the OpenCoweb frameworks are involved (see Section 4.2.2).

At the beginning, a newly created Shape object is added to the canvas and its registerOnCanvas method is called. This, in turn, calls the addShape method of CanvasView. Then, the add action is published via calling publishShapeAdd on the CanvasView. This leads to an involvement of CanvasController by calling its localAddShape method. Thereupon, CanvasController gets the data from the Shape by calling Shape's getData method, which returns the *model* of the shape. CanvasController then adds this *model* to the CanvasModel by invoking the addShape method.

---

37 Table 4.3 is based on http://opencoweb.org/ocwdocs/intro/openg.html (accessed 20/07/2012).

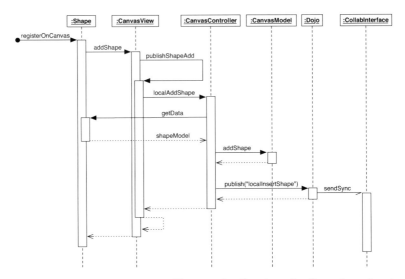

Figure 4.23.: Sequence Diagram Showing the Creation of a Shape by a Local
        User

After that, `CanvasController` publishes the add action to remote users. It is
done by using the publication mechanism of `Dojo`. It calls the `publish` method
of `Dojo` and passes it the `localInsertShape` message. This message is delivered
to the OpenCoweb collaboration Interface via `Dojo`, as `CollabInterface` subscribes to this message. The `CollaborationController` class (see Figure 4.21)
is responsible for establishing this subscription when *ProtoColl* starts. The
`sendSync` method of the `CollabInterface` object is called and asynchronously
transmits the collaboration message to remote users. After that, all methods
return.

For synchronization purposes, *ProtoColl* listens for collaboration messages
sent by remote users. The creation of a shape by a remote user is shown in
the sequence diagram in Figure 4.24. An object of the class `CollabInterface`
gets an asynchronous collaboration message and publishes this via the Dojo
publication mechanism. It calls `publish` on `Dojo` and passes the message

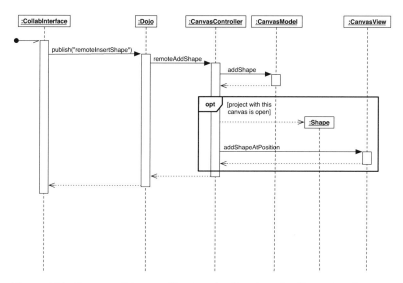

Figure 4.24.: Sequence Diagram Showing the Creation of a Shape by a Remote User

remoteInsertShape. As the CanvasController object has registered for this message, Dojo calls its remoteAddShape method. CanvasController then adds the *model* of the shape to the CanvasModel via the addShape method. If the project is currently open by the user, a new Shape object, which draws the shape on the canvas, is created. This shape is then added to the CanvasView at a specific position via the addShapeAtPosition method. If the project is not opened by the current user, the methods return directly.

5. Evaluation

The artifacts, which have been developed during design science research, should be evaluated in order to examine if they serve the purpose. This evaluation of the developed method and tool is described in this chapter. In the first section, the context of the evaluation is introduced and two propositions, which are evaluated, are derived from theory. The next section describes how the evaluation was conducted. Finally, the last section in this chapter reports the evaluation results.

5.1. Evaluation Context

In their research framework of design science, March and Smith (1995) discuss the different research activities *build, evaluate, theorize, justify*, which are performed in design science research for all cases of different research outputs (constructs, models, methods, instantiations) of design science (March and Smith, 1995) (see Section 2.4). For the evaluation of methods, they consider the following four properties as important:

- Operationality (the ability to perform the intended task or the ability of humans to effectively use the method if it is not algorithmic);

- efficiency;

- generality;

- ease of use.

When evaluating instantiations March and Smith (1995) propose that the following aspects should be considered:

- Efficiency of the artifact;

- effectiveness of the artifact;

- impacts on the environment;

- impacts on its users.

As the method and the mockup tool described in 4.1 and 4.2 correspond to the research outputs *method* and *instantiation*, the above characteristics should be considered as a general framework for the evaluation. The general applicability of the method has been shown to some extent through continuous usage of the prototypical implementation of the tool and the preliminary assessment of the design implications (see Section 3.2), which considered aspects like operationality or ease of use. In the following, propositions based on the constructs of the theories which informed the design parameters of the method and its instantiation, should be developed.

As shown in Chapter 3, the theoretical concept of boundary objects and two theories were used to inform the design of the method and the tool: the Media Synchronicity Theory by Dennis et al. (2008) and the Cognitive-Affective Model of Organizational Communication for Designing IT by Te'eni (2001). As boundary objects (see Section 3.1.1) serve as mediators between different groups of practice, they establish a better *common understanding* of a problem (Subrahmanian et al., 2003). In the specific case of this work, the GUI prototypes play the role of boundary objects. The prototypes represent requirements in a visual form and link to textual descriptions of requirements. Hence, they should facilitate the common understanding of these requirements.

The Media Synchronicity Theory (see Section 3.1.3) explains why different types of communication processes (conveyance and convergence processes) fit best with either synchronous or asynchronous media and thus lead to a better communication performance[1]. Dennis et al. (2008) define communication performance as the development of a *shared understanding*. As discussed in Section 3.1.3, the new method and tool support, both, synchronous and asynchronous collaboration on prototypes in order to account for requirements engineering tasks that require conveyance and convergence processes. Thus, also the design decisions informed by this theory focus on improving the shared and common understanding of the requirements.

The Cognitive-Affective Model of Organizational Communication for Designing IT (see Section 3.1.2) by Te'eni (2001) is a comprehensive model, relating communication process inputs, cognitive-affective communication processes, communication strategies, and the impact of communication. The communication impact covers *mutual understanding*[2] and relationship[3]. In situations that involve high cognitive complexity the model of Te'eni (2001) suggests contextualization as a suitable communication strategy to improve communication impact.

In the context of the method and tool for distributed requirements prototyping, which implies tasks of high cognitive complexity, contextualization techniques are implemented as the possibility to link prototypes to other prototypes or to other artifacts in the software engineering process. In particular, these artifacts can be documents that contain specifications of requirements. As stakeholders involved in the software engineering process are able to trace

---

1 In their 1999 conference paper Dennis and Valacich (1999) call communication performance also *communication effectiveness*.

2 Mutual understanding: The communicative act is judged to be comprehensible and true (Te'eni, 2001).

3 Relationship: The communicative act is judged to be trustworthy and appropriate (Te'eni, 2001).

the relationships between prototypes or relate prototypes to other information (e.g., a detailed specification of data structures used by a data entry mask represented in a prototype), this context information enables them to get a more detailed picture about the requirements represented by the prototypes. Hence, this improves their shared understanding of the requirements.

As the theoretical concepts inform the design of the new method and tool in order to improve its performance in the requirements engineering process, the evaluation of the method and tool should examine the performance constructs explained by the theoretical concepts. The concept of boundary objects can be understood as means of improving *common understanding* between groups. The explained construct of the Media Synchronicity Theory is *shared understanding*, which is equivalent to the explained construct of Cognitive-Affective Model of Organizational Communication for Designing IT, called *mutual understanding*. Hence, proposition P1 should be defined as:

- **P1:** *The method and tool developed in this work improves the shared understanding of the requirements between the stakeholders in the distributed requirements engineering process.*

Prototypes represent boundary objects that act as mediators between stakeholders as discussed in Section 3.1.1. As proposed by proposition P1, this should lead to an improved shared understanding of the requirements. Moreover, this should influence the efficiency of the collaboration between stakeholders positively. As a common ground between the stakeholders is facilitated, less misunderstandings should happen, which leads to less rework. Thus, effort decreases and the efficiency of the collaboration increases.

When a task demands communication processes of convergence, the Media Synchronicity Theory proposes that synchronous media shows a higher communication performance. Dennis et al. (2008) argue, that interaction is beneficial for sensemaking during this process and that convergence is reached more *efficiently*:

> *"We propose that for communication performance on convergence processes, higher levels of media synchronicity will be beneficial to support the interactive give-and-take required for sensemaking strategies, leading to more efficient convergence."* (Dennis et al., 2008, p. 582)

As convergence processes play an important role in requirements negotiation, the method and tool developed in this work supports synchronous collaboration. Prototypes can be modified by all stakeholders who take part in the virtual meeting. Hence, it can be assumed that the usage of the method and tool improves the *collaboration efficiency*. This argument is also supported by a study on requirements negotiation by Damian et al. (2008). It showed that teams, which used asynchronous text-based discussions first to achieve a common ground and used synchronous videoconferencing afterwards, performed in a more efficient way than teams, which did not used asynchronous communication.

Damian et al. (2008) used the argument by Robert and Dennis (2005), which also significantly influenced the Media Synchronicity Theory by Dennis et al. (2008), that media that shows strong information transmission capabilities, often lacks information processing capabilities. Successful requirements negotiation needs the processing of large amounts of information in the first place. Asynchronous communication supports this processing better than synchronous communication, as stakeholders can process and research information about requirements at their own pace. Thus, it is more efficient that teams communicate asynchronously before having synchronous requirements negotiation meetings.

The method and tool developed in this thesis support the linking of various artifacts with the prototypes (e.g., requirements specifications on wiki pages). This was informed by the Cognitive-Affective Model by Te'eni (2001). As the linking enables the users of the method and tool to get quick access to context information for the prototypes and relate different prototypes to each other, it should improve the efficiency in the requirements engineering process.

When compared to traditional methods in distributed requirements engineering, where sketches are created on paper, whiteboards, PDF[4] or PowerPoint documents, the new method and tool should show improvements in terms of efficiency, as time consuming steps are reduced. Stakeholders do not have to travel to meetings in order to create and discuss prototypes, which saves time and costs. As no traveling is needed for these meetings, they can be conducted more often and in shorter iterations. This helps to resolve issues earlier and more frequently, which reduces misunderstandings and rework.

Furthermore, changes can be incorporated into the prototypes quickly and directly by all participants of the meetings. Hence, waiting times for consolidating changes are reduced. In addition, the prototypes are stored in one single tool, which all stakeholders can access. This means, there is always one current version and no need to send around documents, which can lead to inconsistencies. Also this property should lead to efficiency advantages.

Taking all these arguments into account, a second proposition is proposed:

- **P2:** *The method and tool developed in this work improves the efficiency of the collaboration between the stakeholders in the distributed requirements engineering process.*

---

4 The Portable Document Format (PDF) is a file format for documents, which was developed by Adobe Systems (see `http://www.adobe.com/pdf/`, accessed 09/20/2012).

5.2. Evaluation Design

After the propositions have been developed, the evaluation has to be designed. In order to get a deeper understanding about the complex mechanisms of distributed projects and the possible use of the new method and tool, a qualitative study design has been chosen. Several experts from the software industry have been interviewed. These experts work in a company which develops custom software for business clients. These clients are mainly located in Germany.

The company has one location in Germany, which employs primarily project managers, and several development centers in Ukraine, where software engineers work. In total, it employs 20 people in Germany and 100 people in Ukraine. Thus, the company conducts distributed software development projects, where project managers, developers, and clients are located at several locations in two countries.

The experts who were interviewed are mostly project managers. They conduct frequently the requirements engineering and act as a central interface between the client organization and the development teams. Thus, they are most likely to have fundamental knowledge of the processes, tasks, and challenges of distributed requirements engineering and are able to evaluate new requirements engineering methods and tools. In total, eight experts have been interviewed, who had several years of experience in the software industry (see Table 5.1).

The interviews were semi-structured ones, which provided the possibility to react flexibly on the answers of the interviewees. The interview guideline is shown in Appendix B. The interviews lasted 41 minutes on average, and were conducted in individual face-to-face sessions. At the beginning of each interview, the new method and the tool was explained to the expert in detail. Use cases were shown and the experts were given the possibility to try out the software tool.

Table 5.1.: Industry Experts

Expert	Position	Experience
α	Project manager	4 years
β	Project manager	5 years
γ	Project manager	4 years
δ	Project manager	9 years
ϵ	Project manager	2 years
ζ	Project manager	5 years
η	Director operations	7 years
θ	Creative director	10 years

While looking at the method and tool, the experts were instructed to give answers in comparison to their current work processes. When they involved GUI prototypes in their current processes, these prototypes were often created on paper, whiteboards or within PowerPoint presentations. Furthermore, some experts used the tool Balsamiq (see Table 3.2 in Section 3.4). These prototypes were usually created by the experts themselves and shared via email.

5.3. Evaluation Results

After analyzing the answers of the experts, which were recorded during the interviews, findings pertaining the propositions developed above could be obtained.

5.3.1. Proposition P1 – Shared Understanding

Proposition P1 has been supported during the interviews with the experts. They note that the linking of the prototypes with other artifacts should be beneficial for the understanding of the requirements. The linking can provide extra information, which is stored in other documents and important for implementation. The following statement by expert γ emphasizes this:

"I like the linking. Developers must exactly understand what should happen. They need written text. That's very good." – Expert γ

This contextual information can also be essential for other stakeholders like members of the client organization. After looking at a use case in *ProtoColl*, where contextual information is linked to a mockup of a payment system, which shows the security code on a credit card, expert ϵ notes this in the following statement:

"I am a fan of having further information. Just to have a better understanding. Like for the last numbers on a credit card: the security code. Saying OK, what is a security code? It happens all the time that people do not know what a security code is. And when I have such a client who doesn't know what it is, then I have this link and click on it. I think that this information is important and should be accessible by anyone easily and quickly." – Expert ϵ

Furthermore, the linking can improve traceability and enable stakeholders to see how and by whom the prototypes have been created:

"I'm the project manager, I don't know every requirement in every little detail, and someone gives me such a mockup and I ask myself: where does that come from? Is this a proposal from him or is this a suggestion from our side. And therefore the linking [to other artifacts and stakeholders] is very good. I could tell on which information it is based." – Expert γ

Other opportunities to improve mutual understanding of the requirements in distributed projects are problems that appear due to different cultural backgrounds. A simple example for such a case is given by expert α:

"Of course the linking of the documents is a great possibility. We work in different cultural areas: e.g. Dubai, Saudi Arabia, Ukraine. And sometimes we use elements which the Ukrainians do not know. E.g., a pretzel. Then I could show the Ukrainian developer the pretzel here and link to a document which describes it. And so it improves mutual understanding." – Expert ϵ

In addition to the improvements, which result from linking the prototypes to other artifacts, the experts also affirmed that the use of GUI prototypes in general should improve mutual understanding of the requirements. Expert β stated that the client can get a better picture of the requirements:

"[...] the client can see how it looks like and change all these requirements. And that improves the understanding of them." – Expert β

This idea, that GUI prototypes help stakeholders to better imagine the requirements and thus better understand them, is also noted by expert ϵ

"At the end, the client wants a product and he wants to see the result. But to see the result, there are alignment processes. But imagination is limited. And when I see something like this [mockup], I can imagine [the result] and say ok: we didn't think about this issue. And you think a lot earlier about topics which are extremely important for the client but maybe we don't think about them at the moment because it is not our business. This happens again and again. These are misunderstandings that happen because we think we understood it. And theoretically we did, but the client imagined it differently." – Expert ϵ

Expert ζ provides the following statement on the ability of mockups to improve mutual understanding by helping to translate between the languages of developers and business stakeholders:

> *"The developer and the business often speak different languages. And the mockup can help here. That would improve the common understanding."* – Expert ζ

Moreover, the collaborative work with the prototypes stimulates discussions on issues, where different stakeholders can contribute their specific knowledge:

> *"It has a big influence on the understanding of the requirements, because it shows the workflow of the application and shows if we have all information we need. Is everything defined? Do we have all fields and so on. And the developers have different things in mind, e.g. errors. For example, where in the UI do I report errors to the user? Working collaboratively with them on the mockup is very helpful for the understanding."* – Expert γ

The advantage of these discussions is also underlined by the following statement of expert ϵ. It also shows, that integrating many different people into these discussions, which is facilitated with a lightweight tool, is regarded positively:

> *"The more people are involved, the better the problem is understood. Of course you have to agree in the end. But you have a discussion. And this happens relatively early in the development process."* – Expert ϵ

All these expert opinions support proposition P1 and it can be argued that using the new method and tool improves shared understanding of the requirements in distributed requirements engineering.

5.3.2. Proposition P2 – Collaboration Efficiency

The second proposition P2, which relates to the efficiency, can also be supported with the statements of the experts. This is illustrated in the following. Expert α states, that the new method and tool would avoid many unnecessary turnarounds in the communication process during requirements engineering:

> *"It should make work easier and less error-prone. When you create something together, there is no situation where someone first creates something and then discusses it with someone else. Then the other person is not happy with it and it has to be changed. After that, a third person comes and says: no, you can't do it this way because this is not possible with PHP[5]. So when you would do it on paper, it would take a lot of time. A web session would shorten the distance and avoid errors."* – Expert α

A similar statement of expert β also refers to this efficiency improvement. The expert states that the process would have less waiting times, when synchronous collaborative sessions would be used:

> *"Of course that would be ideal. You just say: OK, look at this link and that's it. I used to export PDFs and send them via email. Eventually a reply came: no, we want it a bit different. And this tool would make everything faster and you know instantly the reaction [...] You save time for communication overhead. You can show someone something quickly. With this you save a lot of time. With all the export and sending, sometimes it takes a day until someone replies. You save time because you can communicate quickly."* – Expert β

---

5 PHP: Hypertext Preprocessor (PHP) is a programming language which is mainly used for server side web programming (see `http://www.php.net/`, accessed 09/05/2012).

Expert ϵ also thinks that in many situations synchronous collaboration on the prototypes can be more efficient:

"I had this project for a web site and two new fields should be added. So we made some suggestions and sent it to [the client] and waited a day. Time was lost. Otherwise, we could have said: OK, we have a tool, this one here. Just let us talk half an hour on the phone, if at all, more likely 10 minutes. And I say: look at this, this is the current mockup and drag two lines into it and two fields. Is it OK? But I sent it to them, and they said: OK, the fields must have the same width, and so on. These are all topics which could have been resolved in minutes." – Expert ϵ

The reduction of misunderstandings due to synchronous sessions and the quick access of related information via the links was mentioned by expert γ:

"It increases efficiency by showing misunderstandings very quickly. You lessen the overhead because you enable synchronous work and enable instant visualization and linking to the requirements. You notice quickly when a requirement is not defined, when we have a gap [...] I like the links very much. That saves time, because with one click I can see: OK, there's written something different, the developer must have understood it differently. OK, I just change it and the developer can see it instantly, because it is in the cloud." – Expert γ

Expert ζ also emphasizes the links and the central storage of the prototypes, which help to avoid problems with different versions and out-of-date information:

"The problem is, when you do not work with a central system like this, you always have all these different versions and the different

thoughts, which are not modeled somewhere. And with this tool the links to and from the prototypes lead to current information. When you have documents lying around, you always have to face the problem of non up-to-date information." – Expert ζ

The results from the expert interviews show that proposition P2 can also be supported. The use of the method and the tool should lead to an increase in efficiency. Misunderstandings, unnecessary turnarounds or waiting times, and work with out-of-date information would be reduced. Time would be saved by accessing important context information quickly and easily.

5.3.3. Suggestions for Improvements

The experts made several suggestions to improve *ProtoColl*. They note that user names, which appear in the application, should be shown in different colors for better differentiation of users. Furthermore, elements of prototypes, which are linked and thus clickable, should be colored for better recognizability. Another suggestion is a text generator, which creates dummy text for the text elements. Text should also be formattable, e.g., in bold or italic.

The template library should be searchable for key words. In addition, an overview, which shows how the different application screens are linked, should be available. There should be a dedicated comment functionality, which enables users to comment on the elements of the prototypes. The comments should be hideable and searchable. To avoid switching to external applications, a chat should be integrated into *ProtoColl*. Furthermore, chats could be linked to elements of prototypes. Moreover, user management should be improved. It should be possible to assign roles to users (e.g., administrator, client, developer, project manager) and give these roles specific rights (e.g., view prototypes, edit prototype, view comments, etc.).

To enable the quick access of a specific version of a prototype for, e.g., presentation or export purposes, there should be the possibility to mark specific versions of prototypes as "releases" and name them. Furthermore, it should be possible to record user actions, i.e., clicking on links and navigating between application screens, as videos. Regarding the import and export functionality, *ProtoColl* should be extended to import image and PowerPoint files and export PDF files. Finally, a tighter integration into external applications, e.g., task tracking applications, as a plugin would be desirable.

6. Discussion

6.1. Contributions

This research contributes innovative artifacts, the method and the tool, which were developed considering the findings of theoretical work. Thus, it follows the recommendations of design science by Hevner et al. (2004). In order to support distributed collaboration on GUI prototypes, several design implications have been derived from theoretical concepts, which guided the development of the artifacts (see Section 3.2 in Chapter 4). These design implications determine that the artifacts should support synchronous and asynchronous collaboration. They should also feature the possibility to create links between the prototypes and other external artifacts to provide context information. Moreover, they should support the creation of freehand sketches and provide template GUI widgets.

These design implications lead to a method, which supports the following steps for distributed GUI prototyping: Collecting ideas, refining and enhancing, presenting and negotiating, and tracing requirements during implementation (see Section 4.1.2 in Chapter 4). When collecting ideas, stakeholders collaborate synchronously and often save ideas with freehand sketches. Furthermore, they can link textual requirements in a wiki with the early prototypes. In the refinement step, the stakeholders work mostly asynchronously and enhance and refine the prototypes with more GUI template widgets. When presenting the prototypes, stakeholders meet in a video conference. Sequences of prototypes can be shown and changes can immediately incorporated by all stakeholders. During implementation, it is often helpful for developers to trace back to the prototypes from textual requirements specification. This can improve their understanding of the requirements and the can, in case, contact other stakeholders who created the prototypes. The linking functionality of the artifacts is used for this purpose.

The second artifact, which was developed during this work, is a software tool that is used to implement the method. The tool has been implemented as a lightweight web-based application, which was a design requirement that was identified during the preliminary evaluation. It supports all the other requirements that have been described above. The actions of a user are immediately replicated in all remote users' web browsers, which allows synchronous collaboration. Asynchronous collaboration is possible as the server part of the tool logs all the actions of the users, which enables a history and replay functionality. In addition to this, the tool supports freehand drawing and the creation of complex GUI widget templates, which are stored in a library. Furthermore, predefined standard GUI widgets are available, which can be dragged onto the prototypes and be configured for individual purposes. The tool also provides the possibility to create bidirectional links between the prototypes and other artifacts via simple URLs.

As explained in Section 3.4 in Chapter 4, there is no existing tool, which supports all the functionalities that have been derived from the theoretical concepts and is implemented as a lightweight web-based application (see Table 3.2 in Chapter 4). The tool uses many advanced and also prototypical technologies, which are combined to a new and innovative approach, to make these functionalities possible. These technologies are web technologies as HTML5, JavaScript, SVG, and comet. The tool also builds on frameworks like Dojo and OpenCoweb. It uses operational transformations to ensure that the state of all instances of the tool on the different clients is always consistent (see Section 4.2.2.5 in Chapter 4). As can be seen in Figure 4.20 in Chapter 4, the tool consists of a complex system with client-side applications and server components for synchronization and persistence purposes.

As the design implications for the method and the evaluated propositions are derived from the theoretical concepts and constructs of the boundary objects model (Section 3.1.1), the Media Synchronicity Theory (Section 3.1.3) and the the Cognitive-Affective Model of Organizational Communication for Designing IT (Section 3.1.2), this research also contributes insights into the application of these theoretical works to a new field and supports some of their findings. Thus, it extends the body of knowledge and reports the new findings to the scientific community.

6.2. Implications

The developed artifacts help to reduce severe issues in distributed software projects. As explained in Sections 2.1.1 and 2.2 the issues of poorly understood requirements and inefficient collaboration in distributed projects often lead to delays, extra costs, or complete project failures. As the results of the evaluation show, the method and tool have the potential to reduce these issues. The artifacts help the distributed stakeholders to improve their common understanding of the requirements. Furthermore, they increase the efficiency of the collaboration in distributed software development projects.

When stakeholders get a better common understanding of the requirements, less misunderstandings happen and the probability increases that requirements which actually fit with the users' needs are implemented. Many problems in software projects can be solved early, which prevents rework and delays. This should lead to a higher customer satisfaction and more successful projects.

Another implication is an increase in collaboration efficiency. This should lead to more timely projects and less projects costs.

6.3. Limitations

This research shows several limitations. The evaluation has been conducted with experts of a medium-size company that develops custom made business software, as the support of software development projects in these companies was one major objective of this research. Hence, the applicability of the results of this research for other development projects, e.g., large-size projects, standard software, or entertainment applications, is limited. In principle, the method and tool should also be useful in those kind of projects, but further empirical evidence is needed.

Although the experts had the time to get to know the method and tool in detail before and during the interviews, a longer exposure during a project would possibly reveal further insights. Furthermore, mainly project managers were interviewed, as they played a key role for requirements engineering in the company and collaborated extensively with clients and developers. Although enough insights have been gained, it could be possible that further stakeholders provide other perceptions.

Therefore, the results of the evaluation are initial results, that could be extended in future research. This future work could also involve an experimental evaluation, if problems with the validity of such an approach could be overcome. Another limitation is the that only the tool was evaluated in this thesis. This approach has been chosen, as the tool provides the functionalities to implement the method. Thus, it is the foundation for the execution of the method and tightly connected to it. It is assumed that an evaluation of the execution of the method would reveal similar results.

7. Summary and Outlook

In the first section of this chapter, the results of this thesis are summarized. The second section provides an outlook and suggests possibilities for future research.

7.1. Summary

This thesis follows a design science approach (see Section 2.4) and reports the design and evaluation of a method and tool, which support stakeholders in distributed software development projects to work in collaboration on GUI prototypes. The prototypes act as boundary objects and stimulate the creation of design ideas, visualize possible solutions, transfer knowledge between stakeholders, help to create a shared mental model of requirements, and validate those requirements.

To inform the design of the method, this research makes use of the Cognitive-Affective Model of Organizational Communication for Designing IT (see Section 3.1.2) and the Media Synchronicity Theory (see Section 3.1.3). the theoretical concepts are used to derive several design implications (see Section 3.2), which should assure the effectiveness and efficiency of the method.

The method enables stakeholders in software projects to collaborate asynchronously or synchronously on the prototypes with stakeholders at other locations (see Section 4.1). The prototypes are stored centrally and the current and earlier versions are accessible with little effort. Stakeholders are able to create freehand sketches to provide them the most flexibility for idea creation and can make use of predefined and extensible template GUI widgets for the fast creation of elaborate and detailed prototypes. In order to provide context information to the prototypes (e.g., other artifacts like requirements specifications, task tracking items, wiki pages, architecture design documents), bidirectional links can be created from the prototypes to other artifacts. The steps of the method are outlined in Section 4.1.2. Section 4.1.3 describes how the method can be applied in some example scenarios.

To implement the method, the tool *ProtoColl* has been developed (see Section 4.2). *ProtoColl* consists of a lightweight web-based client application, which communicates with a server backend. The client, which is implemented with more than 15.000 lines of JavaScript code, uses advanced web technologies, like Comet and SVG to provide an interactive and easy to use user experience. The server transmits the actions of a user to other clients to instantly synchronize their states, using operational transformations, and persists these actions to a data base for traceability purposes and asynchronous collaboration (see Section 4.2.2). The architecture of *ProtoColl* has been described in detail in Section 4.2.3. Its functionality from a user perspective has been described in Section 4.2.1.

After the technical design and the implementation of the tool, an evaluation with experts from the software industry has been conducted (see Chapter 5). Two propositions have been derived from the theoretical considerations in Chapter 3. It is proposed that the method and tool improve the shared understanding of the requirements and the efficiency of the collaboration in the distributed requirements engineering process.

The results of the evaluation show that shared understanding and collaboration efficiency are supported by the statements of the industry experts (see

Section 5.3). These experts are mainly project managers in distributed software projects and have to deal with requirements in their daily work. Often, they use GUI prototypes for their work. The experts note that the linking of the prototypes with other artifacts improves the understanding of the requirements, as these links provide valuable context information.

Furthermore, the GUI prototypes are generally seen as very valuable by the experts. They help stakeholders to better imagine requirements and stimulate discussions. When stakeholders are able to create and change the prototypes in synchronous sessions, these meetings clarify many issues and misunderstandings and help to create a shared mental model and understanding of the requirements. An advantage is the possibility to integrate many stakeholders into these meetings, as the tool is lightweight and web-based. This helps to get input from people with a lot of different perspectives.

In addition to support the proposition that *ProtoColl* improves the shared understanding of the requirements, the experts also support the proposition that it increases the collaboration efficiency during distributed requirements engineering. They state that a lot of overhead would be avoided when synchronous collaboration sessions could be used, as many issues can be easily and quickly resolved during those sessions. Waiting times and misunderstandings would be reduced.

Moreover, the experts note that the linking with other artifacts helps to find related information more quickly. In addition, work with various different versions of prototypes is avoided as they are centrally stored and traceable. This eliminates many communication and collaboration problems, which are especially issues in distributed projects, as stakeholders are often not aware of the work of the others and the artifacts they create and update.

7.2. Outlook

In future research projects, the suggestions for improvement by the experts (see Section 5.3) should be implemented. The functionality the experts suggested is very valuable but was not central for this research as this research focused on the functionality that was derived from the design implications in Section 3.2. Nevertheless the implementation could further increase the usefulness of the tool and increase its effectiveness and efficiency in development projects. Hence, it should be implemented to conduct further case studies in industry projects.

Future case studies, where the method and tool is applied in distributed projects, will also be valuable. They have the potential to deliver further insights how stakeholders use the tool in real life projects. Usage scenarios that have not been thought off should be uncovered. Moreover, possible room for improvement could be discovered. Thus, such real life case studies, possibly in various different companies with different types of development projects, are a worthwhile approach for future research.

Furthermore, the integration of the support of other tasks in software development processes seems to be viable. In addition to GUI prototypes, other tasks in software development projects require graphical models, e.g., business process modeling or object oriented design. These exemplary tasks could be supported, if *ProtoColl* would be extended with functionality to create and edit the graphical elements for business processes or UML models.

Another area for future work is the extension of the tool with the possibility to create richer and more dynamic prototypes. For the simulation of dynamic interfaces, functionality could be implemented, which allows widgets to change when the user interacts with them, e.g., expand menus or tree widgets. Also the possibility to enter data and simulate queries on data could be realized. This allows richer prototypes, which better represent the final system.

Moreover, the gap to interface creation tools (e.g. Xcode from Apple[1].), which are used by developers to graphically create runnable user interface code, could be reduced in future work. This can be realized if functionality is included that allows developers to translate the prototypes automatically into models that can be directly used as code for GUIs by the system. An example would be the possibility to generate HTML code from the prototypes that have been modeled with the template widgets in *ProtoColl*.

---

[1] https://developer.apple.com/technologies/tools/ (accessed 10/24/2012)

A. Interview Guideline for the Preliminary Evaluation

- Could you shortly describe your company and your products?

- Could you give some information about your current job, your experience and your background?

- Could you describe the software development process your company uses?

- Is the process distributed? Which locations exist?

- Could you describe how requirements engineering works in your company?

- Which techniques are used for requirements elicitation?

- Which tools are used?

- Who takes part in requirements engineering?

- Which problems occur during requirements elicitation and analysis?

- Do you work with GUI prototypes?

B. Interview Guideline for the Evaluation

- Could you give some information about your current job, your experience and your background?

- Could you shortly describe your company and your products?

- Could you describe the software development process your company uses?

- Could you describe how requirements engineering works in your company?

- Would you use *ProtoColl* in your company?

- For which scenarios do you think *ProtoColl* is most appropriate?

- How could *ProtoColl* possibly affect the understanding of the requirements by distributed stakeholders? Why? Which functionalities could be relevant?

- When would you use the tool asynchronously and when would you use the tool synchronously in meetings?

- Do you think that when the tool is used, the effort to collaborate changes? Why/Why not?

- How could *ProtoColl* be improved?

Bibliography

Ackerman, M., and Halverson, C. (1999). Organizational Memory: Processes, Boundary Objects, and Trajectories. In *Proceedings of the 32nd Annual Hawaii International Conference on Systems Sciences*.

Arnowitz, J., Arent, M., and Berger, N. (2007). *Effective Prototyping for Software Makers*. Morgan Kaufmann.

Aurum, A., and Wohlin, C. (Eds.) (2005a). *Engineering and Managing Software Requirements*. Springer.

Aurum, A., and Wohlin, C. (2005b). Requirements Engineering: Setting the Context. In A. Aurum, and C. Wohlin (Eds.) *Engineering and Managing Software Requirements*, 1–15. Springer.

Barrett, M., and Oborn, E. (2010). Boundary Object Use in Cross-Cultural Software Development Teams. *Human Relations*, *63*(8), 1199–1221.

Beck, K. (1999). Embracing Change with Extreme Programming. *IEEE Computer*, *32*(10), 70–77.

Berander, P., and Andrews, A. (2005). Requirements Prioritization. In A. Aurum, and C. Wohlin (Eds.) *Engineering and Managing Software Requirements*, 69–94. Springer.

Bergman, M., King, J. L., and Lyytinen, K. (2002). Large-Scale Requirements Analysis Revisited: The Need for Understanding the Political Ecology of Requirements Engineering. *Requirements Engineering*, *7*(3), 152–171.

Berry, D. M., and Lawrence, B. (1998). Requirements Engineering. *IEEE Software*, *15*(2), 26–29.

Berson, A. (1996). *Client/Server Architecture*. McGraw-Hill.

Boehm, B. W. (1981). *Software Engineering Economics*. Prentice Hall.

Boland, and Fitzgerald, B. (2004). Transitioning from a Co-Located to a Globally-Distributed Software Development Team: A Case Study at Analog Devices Inc. In *Third International Workshop on Global Software Development, 26th International Conference on Software Engineering*, 4–7.

Bowers, J., and Pycock, J. (1994). Talking Through Design: Requirements and Resistance in Cooperative Prototyping. In *Proceedings of the SIGCHI Conference on Human Factors in Computing Systems: Celebrating Interdependence*, 299–305.

Brandt, E. (2007). How Tangible Mock-Ups Support Design Collaboration. *Knowledge, Technology & Policy*, *20*(3), 179–192.

Brooks, F. (1987). No Silver Bullet: Essence and Accidents of Software Engineering. *IEEE Computer*, *20*(4), 10–19.

Bäumer, D., Bischofberger, W. R., Lichter, H., and Züllighoven, H. (1996). User Interface Prototyping - Concepts, Tools, and Experiences. In *Proceedings of the 18th International Conference on Software Engineering*, 532–541.

Cao, L., and Ramesh, B. (2008). Agile Requirements Engineering Practices: An Empirical Study. *IEEE Software*, *25*(1), 60–67.

Carlile, P. R. (2002). A Pragmatic View of Knowledge and Boundaries: Boundary Objects in New Product Development. *Organization Science*, *13*(4), 442–455.

Chamberlain, S., Sharp, H., and Maiden, N. (2006). Towards a Framework for Integrating Agile Development and User-Centred Design. In P. Abrahamsson,

M. Marchesi, and G. Succi (Eds.) *Extreme Programming and Agile Processes in Software Engineering*, vol. 4044/2006 of *Lecture Notes in Computer Science*, 143–153. Springer.

Charette, R. N. (2005). Why Software Fails. *IEEE Spectrum*, *42*(9), 42–49.

Chau, T., Maurer, F., and Melnik, G. (2003). Knowledge Sharing: Agile Methods vs. Tayloristic Methods. In *Twelfth IEEE International Workshops on Enabling Technologies: Infrastructure for Collaborative Enterprises*, 302–307.

Cheng, B. H. C., and Atlee, J. M. (2007). Research Directions in Requirements Engineering. In *Future of Software Engineering (FOSE'07)*, 285–303.

Choudhary, V. (2007). Software as a Service: Implications for Investment in Software Development. In *40th Annual Hawaii International Conference on System Sciences (HICSS'07)*.

Cockburn, A. (2000). *Writing Effective Use Cases*. Addison-Wesley Professional.

Conchúir, E. , Ågerfalk, P. J., Olsson, H. H., and Fitzgerald, B. (2009). Global Software Development: Where Are the Benefits? *Communications of the ACM*, *52*(8), 127–131.

Coughlan, J., Lycett, M., and Macredie, R. D. (2003). Communication Issues in Requirements Elicitation: A Content Analysis of Stakeholder Experiences. *Information and Software Technology*, *45*(8), 525–537.

Coughlan, J., and Macredie, R. D. (2002). Effective Communication in Requirements Elicitation: A Comparison of Methodologies. *Requirements Engineering*, *7*(2), 47–60.

Crane, D., and McCarthy, P. (2008). *Comet and Reverse Ajax: The Next-Generation Ajax 2.0*. Apress.

Crowston, K., and Kammerer, E. E. (1998). Coordination and Collective Mind in Software Requirements Development. *IBM Systems Journal*, *37*(2), 227–245.

Damian, D. (2007). Stakeholders in Global Requirements Engineering: Lessons Learned from Practice. *IEEE Software*, *24*(2), 21–27.

Damian, D., Lanubile, F., and Mallardo, T. (2008). On the Need for Mixed Media in Distributed Requirements Negotiations. *IEEE Transactions on Software Engineering*, *34*(1), 116–132.

Damian, D., and Zowghi, D. (2003a). An Insight into the Interplay Between Culture, Conflict and Distance in Globally Distributed Requirements Negotiations. In *Proceedings of the 36th Annual Hawaii International Conference on System Sciences (HICSS'03)*, 10–19.

Damian, D., and Zowghi, D. (2003b). Requirements Engineering Challenges in Multi-Site Software Development Organizations. *Requirements Engineering*, *8*(3), 149–160.

Davis, A. (1992). Operational Prototyping: A New Development Approach. *IEEE Software*, *9*(5), 70–78.

Davis, A. M., and Bersoff, E. H. (1991). Impacts of Life Cycle Models on Software Configuration Management. *Communications of the ACM*, *34*(8), 104–118.

Decker, B., Ras, E., Rech, J., Jaubert, P., and Rieth, M. (2007). Wiki-Based Stakeholder Participation in Requirements Engineering. *IEEE Software*, *24*(2), 28–35.

Denger, C., Berry, D., and Kamsties, E. (2003). Higher Quality Requirements Specifications Through Natural Language Patterns. In *Proceedings of the*

IEEE International Conference on Software: Science, Technology and Engineering (SwSTE'03), 80–90.

Dennis, A., Fuller, R., and Valacich, J. S. (2008). Media, Tasks, and Communication Processes: A Theory of Media Synchronicity. *Management Information Systems Quarterly*, *32*(3), 575–600.

Dennis, A., and Valacich, J. (1999). Rethinking Media Richness: Towards a Theory of Media Synchronicity. In *32nd Annual Hawaii International Conference on System Sciences (HICSS'99)*.

Dibbern, J., Winkler, J., and Heinzl, A. (2008). Explaining Variations in Client Extra Costs Between Software Projects Offshored to India. *Management Information Systems Quarterly*, *32*(2), 333–366.

Dieste, O., Juristo, N., and Shull, F. (2008). Understanding the Customer: What Do We Know about Requirements Elicitation? *IEEE Software*, *25*(2), 11–13.

Doolin, B., and McLeod, L. (2012). Sociomateriality and Boundary Objects in Information Systems Development. *European Journal of Information Systems*, *21*(5), 570–586.

Ellis, C. A., and Gibbs, S. J. (1989). Concurrency Control in Groupware Systems. In *Proceedings of the 1989 ACM SIGMOD International Conference on Management of Data*, 399–407.

Espinosa, J. A., Kraut, R. E., Slaughter, S. A., Lerch, J. F., and Herbsleb, J. D. (2002). Shared Mental Models, Familiarity and Coordination: A Multi-Method Study of Distributed Software Teams. In *International Conference on Information Systems*, 425–433. Barcelona, Spain.

Espinosa, J. A., Slaughter, S. A., Kraut, R. E., and Herbsleb, J. D. (2007a). Familiarity, Complexity, and Team Performance in Geographically Distributed Software Development. *Organization Science*, *18*(4), 613–630.

Espinosa, J. A., Slaughter, S. A., Kraut, R. E., and Herbsleb, J. D. (2007b). Team Knowledge and Coordination in Geographically Distributed Software Development. *Journal of Management Information Systems*, *24*(1), 135–169.

Fraser, M., Kumar, K., and Vaishnavi, V. (1991). Informal and Formal Requirements Specification Languages: Bridging the Gap. *IEEE Transactions on Software Engineering*, *17*(5), 454–466.

Geisser, M. (2008). *Requirements Engineering von Informationssystemen: Entwurf einer integrierten Methode für verteilte Szenarios*. Saarbrücken: VDM Verlag Dr. Müller.

Geisser, M., and Hildenbrand, T. (2006). A Method for Collaborative Requirements Elicitation and Decision-Supported Requirements Analysis. In S. Ochoa, and G. Roman (Eds.) *Advanced Software Engineering: Expanding the Frontiers of Software Technology*, 108–122. Springer.

Gervasi, V., and Zowghi, D. (2005). Reasoning About Inconsistencies in Natural Language Requirements. *ACM Transactions on Software Engineering and Methodology*, *14*(3), 277–330.

Glass, R. L. (1998). *Software Runaways: Monumental Software Disasters*. Prentice Hall.

Glass, R. L. (2001). Frequently Forgotten Fundamental Facts About Software Engineering. *IEEE Software*, *18*(3), 112–111.

Gomaa, H., and Scott, D. B. (1981). Prototyping as a Tool in the Specification of User Requirements. In *Proceedings of the 5th International Conference on Software Engineering*, 333–342.

Gotel, O., and Finkelstein, C. (1994). An Analysis of the Requirements Traceability Problem. In *Proceedings of the First International Conference on Requirements Engineering*, 94–101.

Gunaratne, J., Hwong, B., Nelson, C., and Rudorfer, A. (2004). Using Evolutionary Prototypes to Formalize Product Requirements. In *Workshop at the 26th International Conference on Software Engineering (ICSE): Bridging the Gaps Between Software Engineering and Human-Computer Interaction*, 17–20.

Gutwin, C., Penner, R., and Schneider, K. (2004). Group Awareness in Distributed Software Development. In *Proceedings of the 2004 ACM Conference on Computer Supported Cooperative Work*, 72–81.

Hall, T., Beecham, S., and Rainer, A. (2002). Requirements Problems in Twelve Software Companies: An Empirical Analysis. *IEE Proceedings-Software*, *149*(5), 153–160.

Hargreaves, E., Damian, D., Lanubile, F., and Chisan, J. (2004). Global Software Development: Building a Research Community. *ACM SIGSOFT Software Engineering Notes*, *29*(5), 1–5.

Heinrich, L. J., Heinzl, A., and Riedl, R. (2011). *Wirtschaftsinformatik: Einführung und Grundlegung*. Springer, 4th ed.

Herbsleb, J. D., and Mockus, A. (2003). An Empirical Study of Speed and Communication in Globally Distributed Software Development. *IEEE Transactions on Software Engineering*, *29*(6), 481–494.

Herbsleb, J. D., and Moitra, D. (2001). Global Software Development. *IEEE Software*, *18*(2), 16–20.

Herlea, D., and Greenberg, S. (1998). Using a Groupware Space for Distributed Requirements Engineering. In *Proceedings of the 7th IEEE International*

Workshops on Enabling Technologies: Infrastructure for Collaborative Enterprises (WET ICE'98), 57–62.

Hevner, A. R., March, S. T., Park, J., and Ram, S. (2004). Design Science in Information Systems Research. *Management Information Systems Quarterly*, *28*(1), 75–105.

Hickey, A. M., and Davis, A. M. (2004). A Unified Model of Requirements Elicitation. *Journal of Management Information Systems*, *20*(4), 65–84.

Hildenbrand, T. (2008). *Improving Traceability in Distributed Collaborative Software Development: A Design Science Approach*. Peter Lang Verlag.

Hildreth, P., Kimble, C., and Wright, P. (2000). Communities of Practice in the Distributed International Environment. *Journal of Knowledge Management*, *4*(1), 27–38.

Hofmann, H. F. (2000). *Requirements Engineering: A Situated Discovery Process*. Deutscher Universitäts-Verlag.

Hofmann, H. F., and Lehner, F. (2001). Requirements Engineering as a Success Factor in Software Projects. *IEEE Software*, *18*(4), 58–66.

Hsia, P., Davis, A. M., and Kung, D. C. (1993). Status Report: Requirements Engineering. *IEEE Software*, *10*(6), 75–79.

Hsieh, Y. (2006). Culture and Shared Understanding in Distributed Requirements Engineering. In *International Conference on Global Software Engineering (ICGSE'06)*, 101–108.

Hull, E., Jackson, K., and Dick, J. (2010). *Requirements Engineering*. Springer.

IEEE (1990). *IEEE Standard Glossary of Software Engineering Terminology (IEEE Std 610.12-1990)*. IEEE Computer Society.

IEEE (1998). *IEEE Recommended Practice for Software Requirements Specica-*
tion (IEEE Std 830-1998). IEEE Computer Society.

Jiménez, M., Piattini, M., and Vizcaíno, A. (2009). Challenges and Improvements in Distributed Software Development: A Systematic Review. *Advances*
in Software Engineering, 2009.

Kamsties, E. (2005). Understanding Ambiguity in Requirements Engineering.
In A. Aurum, and C. Wohlin (Eds.) *Engineering and Managing Software*
Requirements, 245–266. Springer.

Karlsson, J. (1996). Software Requirements Prioritizing. In *Proceedings of the*
Second International Conference on Requirements Engineering, 110–116.

Karlsson, J., and Ryan, K. (1997). A Cost-Value Approach for Prioritizing
Requirements. *IEEE Software, 14*(5), 67–74.

Karolak, D. W. (1998). *Global Software Development: Managing Virtual Teams*
and Environments. IEEE Computer Society Press.

Katz, A., and Te'eni, D. (2007). The Contingent Impact of Contextualization on
Computer-Mediated Collaboration. *Organization Science, 18*(2), 261–279.

Keil, M., and Carmel, E. (1995). Customer-Developer Links in Software Development. *Communications of the ACM, 38*(5), 33–44.

Komi-Sirviö, S., and Tihinen, M. (2005). Lessons Learned by Participants of
Distributed Software Development. *Knowledge and Process Management,*
12(2), 108–122.

Kommeren, R., and Parviainen, P. (2007). Philips Experiences in Global Distributed Software Development. *Empirical Software Engineering, 12*(6), 647–
660.

Kotonya, G., and Sommerville, I. (1998). *Requirements Engineering: Processes*
and Techniques. Wiley.

Krasner, G., and Pope, S. (1988). A Cookbook for Using the Model-View-Controller User Interface Paradigm in Smalltalk-80. *Journal of Object-Oriented Programming*, *1*(3), 26–49.

Landay, J. A., and Myers, B. A. (1995). Interactive Sketching for the Early Stages of User Interface Design. In *Proceedings of the SIGCHI Conference on Human Factors in Computing Systems*, 43–50. Denver, Colorado, United States.

Landay, J. A., and Myers, B. A. (2001). Sketching Interfaces: Toward More Human Interface Design. *IEEE Computer*, *34*(3), 56–64.

Lee, G., and Xia, W. (2010). Toward Agile: An Integrated Analysis of Quantitative and Qualitative Field Data on Software Development Agility. *Management Information Systems Quarterly*, *34*(1), 87–114.

Leffingwell, D., and Widrig, D. (2000). *Managing Software Requirements: A Unified Approach*. Addison-Wesley Longman Publishing.

Levina, N., and Vaast, E. (2005). The Emergence of Boundary Spanning Competence in Practice: Implications for Implementation and Use of Information Systems. *Management Information Systems Quarterly*, *29*(2), 335–363.

Lichter, H., Schneider-Hufschmidt, M., and Züllighoven, H. (1994). Prototyping in Industrial Software Projects – Bridging the Gap Between Theory and Practice. *IEEE Transactions on Software Engineering*, *20*(11), 825–832.

Lin, J., Newman, M. W., Hong, J. I., and Landay, J. A. (2000). DENIM: Finding a Tighter Fit Between Tools and Practice for Web Site Design. In *Proceedings of the SIGCHI Conference on Human Factors in Computing Systems*, 510–517. The Hague, The Netherlands.

Lindvall, M., Basili, V., Boehm, B., Costa, P., Dangle, K., Shull, F., Tesoriero, R., Williams, L., and Zelkowitz, M. (2002). Empirical Findings in Agile Methods. In D. Wells, and L. Williams (Eds.) *Extreme Programming and Agile Methods - XP/Agile Universe 2002*, vol. 2418 of *Lecture Notes in Computer Science*, 81–92. Springer.

Lloyd, W., Rosson, M., and Arthur, J. (2002). Effectiveness of Elicitation Techniques in Distributed Requirements Engineering. In *Proceedings of the IEEE Joint International Conference on Requirements Engineering*, 311–318.

Loucopoulos, P., and Karakostas, V. (1995). *System Requirements Engineering*. McGraw-Hill.

Luqi, and Royce, W. (1992). Status Report: Computer-Aided Prototyping. *IEEE Software*, *9*(6), 77–81.

Macaulay, L. A. (1996). *Requirements Engineering*. Springer.

Majchrzak, A., Malhotra, A., and John, R. (2005). Perceived Individual Collaboration Know-How Development Through Information Technology–Enabled Contextualization: Evidence from Distributed Teams. *Information Systems Research*, *16*(1), 9–27.

March, S. T., and Smith, G. F. (1995). Design and Natural Science Research on Information Technology. *Decision Support Systems*, *15*(4), 251–266.

Markus, M. L., Majchrzak, A., and Gasser, L. (2002). A Design Theory for Systems That Support Emergent Knowledge Processes. *Management Information Systems Quarterly*, *26*(3), 179–212.

McCurdy, M., Connors, C., Pyrzak, G., Kanefsky, B., and Vera, A. (2006). Breaking the Fidelity Barrier: An Examination of Our Current Characterization of Prototypes and an Example of a Mixed-Fidelity Success. In *Proceedings of the SIGCHI Conference on Human Factors in Computing Systems*, 1233–1242.

Memmel, T., Reiterer, H., and Holzinger, A. (2007). Agile Methods and Visual Specification in Software Development: A Chance to Ensure Universal Access. In C. Stephanidis (Ed.) *Universal Access in Human Computer Interaction. Coping with Diversity*, 453–462. Springer.

Nerur, S., Mahapatra, R., and Mangalaraj, G. (2005). Challenges of Migrating to Agile Methodologies. *Communications of the ACM*, *48*(5), 72–78.

Newman, M. W., and Landay, J. A. (2000). Sitemaps, Storyboards, and Specifications: A Sketch of Web Site Design Practice. In *Proceedings of the 3rd Conference on Designing Interactive Systems: Processes, Practices, Methods, and Techniques*, 263–274. New York, NY, USA.

Newman, M. W., Lin, J., Hong, J. I., and Landay, J. A. (2003). DENIM: An Informal Web Site Design Tool Inspired by Observations of Practices. *Human Computer Interaction*, *18*(3), 259–324.

Niehaves, B. (2007). On Epistemological Diversity in Design Science: New Vistas for a Design-Oriented IS Research. In *Twenty-Eighth International Conference on Information Systems*. Montreal.

Niinimäki, T., Piri, A., Lassenius, C., and Paasivaara, M. (2010). Reflecting the Choice and Usage of Communication Tools in GSD Projects with Media Synchronicity Theory. In *5th IEEE International Conference on Global Software Engineering*, 3–12. Princeton, NJ, USA.

Nuseibeh, B., and Easterbrook, S. (2000). Requirements Engineering: A Roadmap. In *Proceedings of the Conference on The Future of Software Engineering*, 35–46.

Nuseibeh, B., Kramer, J., and Finkelstein, A. (1994). A Framework for Expressing the Relationships Between Multiple Views in Requirements Specification. *IEEE Transactions on Software Engineering*, *20*(10), 760–773.

Paetsch, F., Eberlein, A., and Maurer, F. (2003). Requirements Engineering and Agile Software Development. In *Proceedings of the Twelfth International Workshop on Enabling Technologies: Infrastructure for Collaborative Enterprises*, 308–313.

Paulson, L. (2005). Building Rich Web Applications with Ajax. *Computer*, *38*(10), 14–17.

Pawlowski, S. D., and Robey, D. (2004). Bridging User Organizations: Knowledge Brokering and the Work of Information Technology Professionals. *Management Information Systems Quarterly*, *28*(4), 645–672.

Pawlowski, S. D., Robey, D., and Raven, A. (2000). Supporting Shared Information Systems: Boundary Objects, Communities, and Brokering. In *Proceedings of the Twenty First International Conference on Information Systems*, 329–338.

Pohl, K. (1997). Requirements Engineering. In A. Kent, and J. G. Williams (Eds.) *Encyclopedia of Computer Science and Technology*, vol. 36, supplement 21, 345–386. Marcel Dekker.

Pohl, K. (2010). *Requirements Engineering: Fundamentals, Principles, and Techniques*. Springer, 1st ed.

Pries-Heje, J., Baskerville, R., and Venable, J. (2008). Strategies for Design Science Research Evaluation. In *Proceedings of the 16th European Conference on Information Systems*.

Procaccino, J. D., Verner, J. M., and Lorenzet, S. J. (2006). Defining and Contributing to Software Development Success. *Communications of the ACM*, *49*(8), 79–83.

Ramasubbu, N., and Balan, R. K. (2007). Globally Distributed Software Development Project Performance: An Empirical Analysis. In *Proceedings of the*

the 6th Joint Meeting of the European Software Engineering Conference and the ACM SIGSOFT Symposium on the Foundations of Software Engineering, ESEC-FSE '07, 125–134.

Ramesh, B., Cao, L., Mohan, K., and Xu, P. (2006). Can Distributed Software Development Be Agile? Communications of the ACM, 49(10), 41–46.

Ratanaworabhan, P., Livshits, B., and Zorn, B. G. (2010). JSMeter: Comparing the Behavior of Javascript Benchmarks with Real Web Applications. In Proceedings of the 2010 USENIX Conference on Web Application Development, WebApps'10, 3–3. Berkeley, CA, USA.

Ravid, A., and Berry, D. M. (2000). A Method for Extracting and Stating Software Requirements that a User Interface Prototype Contains. Requirements Engineering, 5(4), 225–241.

Redmiles, D., Van Der Hoek, A., Al-ani, B., Hildenbrand, T., Quirk, S., Sarma, A., Filho, R. S. S., De Souza, C., and Trainer, E. (2007). Continuous Coordination: A New Paradigm to Support Globally Distributed Software Development Projects. Wirtschaftsinformatik, 49(1), 28–38.

Ressel, M., Nitsche-Ruhland, D., and Gunzenhäuser, R. (1996). An Integrating, Transformation-Oriented Approach to Concurrency Control and Undo in Group Editors. In Proceedings of the 1996 ACM Conference on Computer Supported Cooperative Work, CSCW '96, 288–297.

Ricca, F., Di Penta, M., Torchiano, M., Tonella, P., and Ceccato, M. (2007). The Role of Experience and Ability in Comprehension Tasks Supported by UML Stereotypes. In 29th International Conference on Software Engineering, ICSE, 375–384.

Ricca, F., Scanniello, G., Torchiano, M., Reggio, G., and Astesiano, E. (2010). On the Effectiveness of Screen Mockups in Requirements Engineering: Results from an Internal Replication. In Proceedings of the 2010 ACM-IEEE

International Symposium on Empirical Software Engineering and Measurement, ESEM '10.

Rivero, J., Rossi, G., Grigera, J., Burella, J., Luna, E., and Gordillo, S. (2010). From Mockups to User Interface Models: An Extensible Model Driven Approach. In F. Daniel, and F. Facca (Eds.) *Current Trends in Web Engineering*, vol. 6385 of *Lecture Notes in Computer Science*, 13–24. Springer.

Robert, L. P., and Dennis, A. R. (2005). Paradox of Richness: A Cognitive Model of Media Choice. *IEEE Transactions on Professional Communication*, *48*(1), 10–21.

Robertson, J., and Robertson, S. (2000). Requirements Management: A Cinderella Story. *Requirements Engineering*, *5*(2), 134–136.

Robertson, S., and Robertson, J. C. (2006). *Mastering the Requirements Process*. Addison-Wesley Professional, 2 ed.

Royce, W. W. (1970). Managing the Development of Large Software Systems. In *Proceedings of IEEE WESCON*, vol. 26.

Rudd, J., Stern, K., and Isensee, S. (1996). Low vs. High-Fidelity Prototyping Debate. *Interactions*, *3*(1), 76–85.

Saiedian, H., and Dale, R. (2000). Requirements Engineering: Making the Connection Between the Software Developer and Customer. *Information and Software Technology*, *42*(6), 419–428.

Scacchi, W. (2002). Understanding the Requirements for Developing Open Source Software Systems. *IEE Proceedings-Software*, *149*(1), 24–39.

Schwaber, K. (2004). *Agile Project Management with Scrum*. Microsoft Press.

Sengupta, B., Chandra, S., and Sinha, V. (2006). A Research Agenda for Distributed Software Development. In *Proceedings of the 28th International Conference on Software Engineering*, ICSE '06, 731–740.

Sharp, H., Finkelstein, A., and Galal, G. (1999). Stakeholder Identification in the Requirements Engineering Process. In *Proceedings of the 10th International Workshop on Database and Expert Systems Applications. DEXA 99*, 387–391. Florence, Italy.

Sidhavatula, V., and Wendt, A. (2007). Using Mock-ups, a Feature of the Scandinavian Approach to User Involvement in Design. In *Student Interaction Design Research Conference*, 89–92. Ronneby, Sweden.

Simon, H. A. (1996). *The Sciences of the Artificial*. MIT Press.

Snyder, C. (2003). *Paper Prototyping: The Fast and Easy Way to Design and Refine User Interfaces*. Morgan Kaufmann.

Sommerville, I. (2005). Integrated Requirements Engineering: A Tutorial. *IEEE Software*, *22*(1), 16–23.

Sommerville, I. (2007). *Software Engineering*. Addison-Wesley, 8 ed.

Sommerville, I., and Sawyer, P. (1997). *Requirements Engineering: A Good Practice Guide*. Wiley.

Star, S. L., and Griesemer, J. R. (1989). Institutional Ecology, 'Translations' and Boundary Objects: Amateurs and Professionals in Berkeley's Museum of Vertebrate Zoology, 1907-39. *Social Studies of Science*, *19*(3), 387–420.

Stuckenberg, S., and Heinzl, A. (2010). The Impact of the Software-as-a-Service Concept on the Underlying Software and Service Development Processes. *Proceedings of the Pacific Asia Conference on Information Systems (PACIS)*.

Subrahmanian, E., Monarch, I., Konda, S., Granger, H., Milliken, R., and Westerberg, A. (2003). Boundary Objects and Prototypes at the Interfaces of Engineering Design. *Computer Supported Cooperative Work (CSCW)*, *12*(2), 185–203.

Sun, C., Jia, X., Zhang, Y., Yang, Y., and Chen, D. (1998). Achieving Convergence, Causality Preservation, and Intention Preservation in Real-Time Cooperative Editing Systems. *ACM Transactions on Computer-Human Interaction*, *5*(1), 63–108.

Sääksjärvi, M., Lassila, A., and Nordström, H. (2005). Evaluating the Software as a Service Business Model: From CPU Time-Sharing to Online Innovation Sharing. In *Proceedings of the IADIS International Conference e-Society*, 177–186.

Te'eni, D. (2001). Review: A Cognitive-Affective Model of Organizational Communication for Designing IT. *Management Information Systems Quarterly*, *25*(2), 251–312.

The Standish Group (2009). CHAOS Summary 2009.
URL http://www.standishgroup.com/newsroom/chaos_2009.php

van Lamsweerde, A. (2000). Requirements Engineering in the Year 00: A Research Perspective. In *Proceedings of the 22nd International Conference on Software Engineering*, ICSE '00, 5–19.

van Lamsweerde, A., Darimont, R., and Letier, E. (1998). Managing Conflicts in Goal-Driven Requirements Engineering. *IEEE Transactions on Software Engineering*, *24*(11), 908–926.

Verner, J., Cox, K., Bleistein, S., and Cerpa, N. (2005). Requirements Engineering and Software Project Success: An Industrial Survey in Australia and the US. *Australian Journal of Information Systems*, *13*(1).

Walker, M., Takayama, L., and Landay, J. A. (2002). High-Fidelity or Low-Fidelity, Paper or Computer? Choosing Attributes When Testing Web Prototypes. In *Human Factors and Ergonomics Society Annual Meeting Proceedings*, vol. 46, 661–665. Baltimore, MD, USA.

Walls, J. G., Widmeyer, G. R., and El Sawy, O. A. (1992). Building an Information System Design Theory for Vigilant EIS. *Information Systems Research*, *3*(1), 36–59.

Wenger, E. (1998). *Communities of Practice*. Cambridge University Press.

Wiegers, K. (2003). *Software Requirements*. Microsoft Press, 2nd ed.

Wiegers, K. (2006). *More About Software Requirements: Thorny Issues and Practical Advice*. Microsoft Press.

Wong, Y. Y. (1992). Rough and Ready Prototypes: Lessons from Graphic Design. In *Posters and Short Talks of the 1992 SIGCHI Conference on Human Factors in Computing Systems*, 83–84. Monterey, California.

Xia, S., Sun, D., Sun, C., Chen, D., and Shen, H. (2004). Leveraging Single-User Applications for Multi-User Collaboration: The Coword Approach. In *Proceedings of the 2004 ACM Conference on Computer Supported Cooperative Work*, CSCW '04, 162–171.

Zowghi, D., and Coulin, C. (2005). Requirements Elicitation: A Survey of Techniques, Approaches, and Tools. In A. Aurum, and C. Wohlin (Eds.) *Engineering and Managing Software Requirements*, 19–46. Springer.

ENTSCHEIDUNGSUNTERSTÜTZUNG FÜR ÖKONOMISCHE PROBLEME

Herausgegeben von Christian Becker, Wolfgang Gaul, Armin Heinzl, Alexander Mädche und Martin Schader

Band 1 Ingo Böckenholt: Mehrdimensionale Skalierung qualitativer Daten. Ein Instrument zur Unterstützung von Marketingentscheidungen. 1989.

Band 2 Jürgen Joseph: Arbeitswissenschaftliche Aspekte der betrieblichen Einführung neuer Technologien am Beispiel von Computer Aided Design (CAD). Felduntersuchung zur Ermittlung arbeitswissenschaftlicher Empfehlungen für die Einführung neuer Technologien. 1990.

Band 3 Eva Schönfelder: Entwicklung eines Verfahrens zur Bewertung von Schichtsystemen nach arbeitswissenschaftlichen Kriterien. 1992.

Band 4 Michael Bargl: Akzeptanz und Effizienz computergestützter Dispositionssysteme in der Transportwirtschaft. Empirische Studien zur Implementierungsforschung von Entscheidungsunterstützungssystemen am Beispiel computergestützter Tourenplanungssysteme. 1994.

Band 5 Reinhold Decker: Analyse und Simulation des Kaufverhaltens auf Konsumgütermärkten. Konzeption eines modell- und wissensorientierten Systems zur Auswertung von Paneldaten. 1994.

Band 6 Wolfgang Gaul / Martin Schader (Hrsg.): Wissensbasierte Marketing-Datenanalyse. Das WIMDAS-Projekt. 1994.

Band 7 Daniel Baier: Konzipierung und Realisierung einer Unterstützung des kombinierten Einsatzes von Methoden bei der Positionierungsanalyse. 1994.

Band 8 Ulrich Lutz: Preispolitik im internationalen Marketing und westeuropäische Integration. 1994.

Band 9 Kirsten Petersen: Design eines Courseware-Entwicklungssystems für den computerunterstützten universitären Unterricht. CULLIS-Teilprojekt I. 1996.

Band 10 Stefan Neumann: Einsatz von Interactive Video im computerunterstützten universitären Unterricht. CULLIS Teilprojekt II. 1996.

Band 11 Eberhard Aust: Simultane Conjointanalyse, Benefitsegmentierung, Produktlinien- und Preisgestaltung. 1996.

Band 12 Peter Heydebreck: Technologische Verflechtung. Ein Instrument zum Erreichen von Produkt- und Prozeßinnovationserfolg. 1996.

Band 13 Michael Pesch: Effiziente Verkaufsplanung im Investitionsgütermarketing. 1997.

Band 14 Frank Wartenberg: Entscheidungsunterstützung im persönlichen Verkauf. 1997.

Band 15 Thomas Lechler: Erfolgsfaktoren des Projektmanagements. 1997.

Band 16 Alexandre Saad: Anbahnung und Erfolg von europäischen kooperativen F&E-Projekten. Eine empirische Analyse anhand von ESPRIT-Projekten. 1998.

Band 17 Michael Löffler: Integrierte Preisoptimierung. 1999.

Band 18 Frank Säuberlich: KDD und Data Mining als Hilfsmittel zur Entscheidungsunterstützung. 2000.

INFORMATIONSTECHNOLOGIE UND ÖKONOMIE

(Neuer Reihentitel ab Band 19)

www.peterlang.com